YOU ARE
AWESOME

NEIL PASRICHA
GET NEIL'S LATEST WRITING FOR FREE AT
WWW.NEIL.BLOG/NEWSLETTERS

You are what you eat.

And you are what you read.

Are you hungry?

Let's go.

You Are Awesome

"With all the world throws at us, resilience is now a precious commodity, and it's the underpinning of this terrifically helpful book by Neil Pasricha. *You Are Awesome* is more than a boost for your self-esteem—it's a perspective-setter for failure and success, and an homage to the amazing reserves of the human soul."

MITCH ALBOM, author of *Finding Chika* and
The Five People You Meet in Heaven

"Do you have thin skin like the rest of us? The tool you need is *resilience*. Let this deeply researched book be your step-by-step guide."

SUSAN CAIN, author of *Quiet*

"Neil was an incredibly quiet, shy, and curious student in my classroom over thirty years ago. I have long retired from teaching and am now watching as he becomes the teacher for me and many others. This book is a guidebook for those establishing careers and raising families. But it's also for those of us in later years who are still seeking to set aside precious time for people and activities we love and who face a whole new set of challenges. As always, Neil's glass is half full and his enthusiasm for living is truly infectious."

MRS. STELLA DORSMAN, Neil's third-grade teacher

"I have been through struggle. I have been through loss. And I have had to get stronger. Resilience is a muscle that hurts to build. What would have made it easier? Neil's words. This book. A recipe for thickening our skin in thin-skinned times."

JAMES FREY, author of *A Million Little Pieces*

"I give this book five stars! Actually star's rating be so insufficient when it comes to Neil Pasricha, I give him all the universe for being the Sun, the light, the hope the happiness for so many of us in life with his extraordinary efforts in writing this book, what a book, seems a bible of happiness, a Google map of revisiting life! Thanks for yet another wonder Neil . . ."

VISHWAS AGGRAWAL, the world's greatest Uber driver with a 4.99 rating and over 5,000 rides

"Pick up this book for its gloriously self-affirming title—after all, you *are* awesome!—and stay for its wise and transformative advice. Writing in his usual engaging style, Pasricha will challenge you to build resilience, get out of your own way, and pursue a life of accomplishment and meaning."

DANIEL H. PINK, author of *When, Drive,* and *To Sell Is Human*

"*You Are Awesome* is the exact book we need to offset the constant negativity that comes in and out of our life each day. Pasricha forces us to look within and become the best we can be by controlling our inner voice and blocking all the distractions."

MICHAEL LOMBARDI, former NFL executive with three Super Bowl rings and host of *The GM Shuffle*

"This utterly charming book will put a smile on your face and a skip in your step."

ADAM GRANT, *New York Times* bestselling author of *Give and Take, Originals,* and *Option B,* and host of the TED podcast *WorkLife*

"With Neil's signature style of humor, research, whimsy, and insight, *You Are Awesome* touches a chord and shows us the power of combining optimism and resilience to create more meaning at work, school, and home."

SHAWN ACHOR, *New York Times* bestselling author of *Big Potential*

"There are few things more certain in all aspects of life than set-backs! Finding the resilience to not just cope but also take these in your stride and ultimately learn from them is a critical skill in today's unpredictable world. Neil's book provides an invaluable framework and tool kit. Full of practical ideas and suggestions, supported by personal anecdotes and stories that bring them to life. Neil has done it again, producing a personal, practical, and universal guide to life."

DAVID CHEESEWRIGHT, former president and CEO, Walmart International

"Neil is the happiness mixologist. He combines an insight for awesome, a dry sense of humor, hard-earned wisdom, and just the right amount of science, shakes it all together vigorously, and then pours you a libation you can toast to life that's rich, resilient, and deeply delicious."

MICHAEL BUNGAY STANIER, author of *The Coaching Habit*

"A brilliant book, generous, heartfelt, and true. Neil is going to help you change your life."

SETH GODIN, *New York Times* bestselling author of *Linchpin* and *Tribes*

"A playful, yet powerful path from anxious to awesome. Pasricha blends science, story and a healthy dose of humor to deliver tools and strategies that cultivate resilience in a world that's never needed it more."

JONATHAN FIELDS, author, podcaster, and creator of Good Life Project® and Sparketype™

"No one knows 'awesome' like Neil Pasricha, and here he explores how we can make our very lives more awesome. With real-life stories and a conversational style, he shows how we can move forward in the face of challenge to make our days more intentional and joyful."

GRETCHEN RUBIN, author of *The Happiness Project* and *Outer Order, Inner Calm*

ALSO BY NEIL PASRICHA

BOOKS

The Happiness Equation
The Book of (Holiday) Awesome
The Book of (Even More) Awesome
The Book of Awesome

PICTURE BOOK

Awesome Is Everywhere

JOURNALS

Two Minute Mornings
The Journal of Awesome

PODCAST

3 Books with Neil Pasricha

TED TALKS

"How Do You Maximize Your Tiny, Short Life?"
"The 3 A's of Awesome"

SITES

neil.blog
3books.co
globalhappiness.org
1000awesomethings.com

YOU ARE AWESOME

How to Navigate Change, Wrestle with Failure, and Live an Intentional Life

NEIL PASRICHA

GALLERY BOOKS

New York   London   Toronto   Sydney   New Delhi

Gallery Books
An Imprint of Simon & Schuster, Inc.
1230 Avenue of the Americas
New York, NY 10020

First Gallery Books hardcover edition November 2019

GALLERY BOOKS and colophon are registered trademarks of Simon & Schuster, Inc.

For information about special discounts for bulk purchases,
please contact Simon & Schuster Special Sales at
1-866-506-1949 or business@simonandschuster.com.

The Simon & Schuster Speakers Bureau can bring authors to your live event. For
more information or to book an event, contact the Simon & Schuster Speakers
Bureau at 1-866-248-3049 or visit our website at www.simonspeakers.com.

Manufactured in USA

3   5   7   9   10   8   6   4   2

Library of Congress Cataloging-in-Publication Data has been applied for.

ISBN 978-1-9821-3588-1
ISBN 978-1-9821-3590-4 (ebook)

I love that you're reading all the small print right now. Nobody reads this page! Well, nobody except us. You probably read shampoo bottles too, right? I love that. I think it means you care. And that you notice things. And I think it means we're going to get along great.

CONTENTS

CONTENTS

YOU ARE

AWESOME

You Need to Be More Resilient

There's an old Taoist fable about a farmer with one horse. Have you heard it? It goes like this:

A farmer had only one horse. One day, his horse ran away.

His neighbors said, "I'm so sorry. This is such bad news. You must be so upset."

The man just said, "We'll see."

A few days later, his horse came back with twenty wild horses following. The man and his son corralled all twenty-one horses.

His neighbors said, "Congratulations! This is such good news. You must be so happy!"

The man just said, "We'll see."

One of the wild horses kicked the man's only son, breaking both his legs.

His neighbors said, "I'm so sorry. This is such bad news. You must be so upset."

The man just said, "We'll see."

The country went to war, and every able-bodied young man was drafted to fight. The war was terrible and killed every young man, but the farmer's son was spared since his broken legs prevented him from being drafted.

His neighbors said, "Congratulations! This is such good news. You must be so happy!"

The man just said, "We'll see . . ."

What is up with this crazy farmer, right?

Well, what's up with this crazy farmer is that he has truly developed resilience. He has built up his resilience. He is resilient! He's steady, he's ready, and whatever the future brings, we all know he's going to stare it straight in the face with eyes that scream, "Bring it on."

The farmer has come to understand that every skyrocketing pleasure or stomach-churning defeat defines not *who he is* but simply *where he is.*

The farmer knows that what happens in life only serves to help him see where he is and decide which way to go next.

The farmer knows every end is a beginning.

Whenever I read the fable of the farmer with one horse I sort of picture one of those inflatable clown punching bags that stands in the corner at a five-year-old's birthday party.

Do you know the ones I mean?

They look like this:

Pop him in the nose! He goes down. He gets back up. Knock him to the ground with a violent bear hug! He goes down. He gets back up. Deliver a dirty karate kick to the side of his head? He goes down.

And he gets back up.

Resilience.

In my journey to think, write, and speak about how we live an intentional life—while always wrestling with my own demons as I do so—this concept of resilience has quickly moved front and center with the volume blaring.

I wasn't looking for it!

Ten years ago my wife left me and my best friend took his own life, and I channeled that heartbreak into the simple practice of writing one awesome thing a day on a blog called *1000 Awesome Things*. That blog turned into my first book.

The Book of Awesome is all about **gratitude**.

Five years later I met and fell in love with Leslie, and we got married. She told me she was pregnant on the flight home from our honeymoon. When we landed I started writing a long letter to my unborn child on how to live a happy life. That letter turned into my last book.

The Happiness Equation is all about **happiness**.

And now I'm saying that resilience has moved front and center and become loud and clear.

Why?

Because resilience is a skill we now have in very short supply. Not many of us have been through famines or wars or, let's be honest, any form of true scarcity. We have it all! And the side effect is that we no longer have the tools to handle failure or even perceived failure. These days when we fall we just lie on the sidewalk crying. We are turning into an army of porcelain dolls.

After a speech I gave recently a breathless fiftysomething ran up to me and asked a question that represented what I'm getting asked everywhere:

> My son was captain of the high school football team! He graduated with honors from Duke! And he called me last night crying again because his boss sent him a rude email! What is going on with him? What is going on with us? And what do we do about it?

What *is* going on with us?

We are living in a world where we no longer bend—we break. When we spill, we splatter. When we crack, we shatter. The *New York Times* reports that one in three adolescents has clinical anxiety. Cell phones show us we're never good enough. Yesterday's butterflies are tomorrow's panic attacks. And what about rates of depression, loneliness, and suicide? All rising!

We just can't handle it.

Today we need to learn the skills the farmer had in spades. And we need to learn them fast. Volatility, uncertainty, and complexity are accelerating. Change? Constant. Latest disruption? Getting disrupted. Meanwhile we know relationships will always spin and swerve and life always, always, always has other plans.

What do we need?

To be like the farmer.

What do we want?

To be like the farmer.

We need to take all the uncertainty and failure and change coming at us and use it as momentum that slingshots us forward and forward and forward.

You Are Awesome is all about **resilience**.

It is a series of nine research-backed secrets, shared through personal stories, on how we can move from change-resistant to change-ready, failure-prone to failure-proof, thin-skinned to thick-skinned, and anxious to awesome.

Life is tiny and fragile and beautiful and precious.

And we really are awesome.

All we need are a few directional arrows to get us back on track whenever we fall off course.

This is a book of nine arrows.

I hope you like it.

Neil

Add a Dot-Dot-Dot

M y mom was born in Nairobi, Kenya, in 1950.

Growing up the youngest of eight kids in a small house off the downtown core, she was quiet, shy, and always the baby.

Back when my mom was born, Kenya had a black majority, a brown minority, and a white cream on top. Kenyan natives, the East Indian class imported to get the economy chugging, and the British colonialists who ran the whole show.

That East Indian class included my mom's dad who moved from Lahore, India, to Nairobi in the 1930s to help build the railroad.

The Brits took over Kenya in the late 1800s and the country didn't gain independence until the mid-1960s so it was very much a British-ruled country when my mom was born. White people running the show. White people running the government. White people running the best schools.

My mom wasn't born a white person.

So she wasn't born the *right* person.

And she wasn't born the right gender, either.

What do I mean?

I mean my grandparents had seven kids before my mom was born. Four girls and three boys. As my mom and her sisters tell it, my grandparents were desperately hoping for a final boy to even their numbers out and give them a solid four-four split.

Boys were the prized possession in the culture. All everybody wanted.

For generations there was more money for male education and training, which meant men were financially self-sufficient. Women, on the other hand, were dependent on husbands opening wallets every Sunday to dole out shillings to buy groceries and clothes for the family. Women also traditionally "married out" and joined their husbands' families, taking care of their in-laws instead of their own parents. So having a son provided a *cultural pension* long before real pensions existed. No old-age checks once a month! Just your daughter-in-law cooking you curried lentils and serving you chai.

Even worse, the culture compensated men further by providing a *dowry*. What's a dowry? I didn't understand it growing up but a dowry is an ancient and archaic gift given by the bride's parents to the groom's parents as if to say "Thank you for taking our daughter off our hands."

By the way, I really do mean *ancient*. Even one of the world's oldest texts, the Code of Hammurabi, dating from almost four thousand years ago, discusses dowries in this way, as gifts for the

4

groom's family. And I do mean *gift*. A dowry often includes jewelry, property, and big piles of cash, resulting in a massive financial burden for anyone with a daughter to marry off.

When my grandparents had my mom, all those additional costs and burdens sank in. It breaks my heart to think about my mom opening her newborn eyes, slowly soaking in the sea of faces in front of her, and what was the first thing she probably saw?

Everyone's disappointment.

How was that family burden, that sense of not being wanted, communicated to my mother? The way deep cultural norms are often communicated—like a heavy, invisible blanket pushing down on her, a force she couldn't see but felt in her bones.

When a boy was born, friends and neighbors would say "*Badhaee ho!*" It meant "Wonderful, great, congratulations!" And when a girl was born? "*Chalo koi nahi.*" What's the translation? "Keep going. Soldier on. *Oh well*—you have to keep moving."

As my mom described it, there was a fatalist feeling of closure and finality over everything. "My life was set out," she told me. "It was decided." Gender, culture, and traditions all pointed to a well-worn finish line she could see in her future. Her life seemed like a sentence. Something preordained and punishing.

No sense of possibility, no options . . . no dot-dot-dot.

Just the end. A full stop.

As she got older, my mom watched her older sisters finishing the same sentence ahead of her, plucked from the family home one by one, married off to a man chosen by her parents, to provide him with children and home cooking while taking care of him and his parents. In the face of a life sentence ending in a full stop, my mom had a choice to make: Would she ever see past the period?

What about you?

Do you ever feel like you don't have options?

Do you ever feel like you don't have a choice?

Do you ever see the period at the end of your sentence?

We all have this feeling sometimes.

We all sometimes feel a fatalist feeling of closure and finality in the sentence of our lives. Maybe it's growing up in a male-dominated culture without any visible options. Maybe it's taking care of a sick family member and always putting yourself last. Maybe it's feeling trapped in your job after twenty years of education and a suffocating pile of debt. Maybe your family is living in a country where your visa application to join them keeps getting rejected. Maybe they won't promote you. Maybe they won't release you.

What do you do when you can see the future on the path you're walking on but you don't like where it's leading?

Well, there's a crucial mindset to adopt. It's not about giving up. And it's not about turning around and running away. Because we both know life isn't that simple. Commencement speech advice doesn't always work. *Follow your heart! Do what you love!*

"My heart said follow him. And he dumped me."

"I want to do what I love. But I have bills, responsibilities, and other people."

Sometimes the hardest thing to do is simply making the decision to keep going.

Sometimes the hardest thing to do is simply making the

decision to continue to breathe, continue to move, continue to function, continue to operate.

A period means giving in to life's circumstances, relenting in the face of things that look immovable, things that look impossible, things that look too painful.

A period is giving in.

What we need to hold on to in our hearts is the quiet courage to change the punctuation. What we need to hold on to is the idea that resilience means seeing the free will that exists just past the period.

We need to hold on to a desire to see past that full stop.

To see past the period.

And add a dot-dot-dot.

1

A 500-year-old invention we can use today

In grammatical terms, that dot-dot-dot is called an ellipsis.

Dr. Anne Toner is a Cambridge University academic who spent years studying the history of the ellipsis. No, I'm not joking. But there is good news. She found it! Yes, the first time the famous dot-dot-dot appears is in the 1588 English translation of Roman dramatist Terence's play *Andria*.

Let's pause for a moment to stare at a bit of blurry calligraphy from half a millennium ago. The first-ever ellipsis. Fellow history and trivia nerds, turn the page to see the amber-encapsulated marvel . . .

Act. 5. Scen. 3.

The Argument.

SIMO sharply rebuketh his sonne: who confessing his fault, submitteth himselfe wholy vnto his fathers pleasure. Chremes endeuoreth to appease theatreame Rage of Simo.

Pamphilus, Simo, Chremes.

Who calles me? O I am vndone, it is
my father.
Si. What saiest thou? thou arrand - - - -
Chr. Fie, go to the matter, and ceaso
your euill language.
Si. Yea as though there could be any
name to ill for this fellow. Now sirra, do you say the
same to? Is Glycerie free bone of this Citie?
Pamph. So it is reported.
Si.

Look like small potatoes? Well, let's see if we can come up with a new punctuation mark the whole world will use in five hundred years. It's not easy. But there was help. Ben Jonson began using it in his plays soon after and then that old bard Bill Shakespeare joined in the fray. Boom! That was the Middle Ages equivalent of getting retweeted by Oprah. The ellipsis then moved from there all the way up to Virginia Woolf and Joseph Conrad. Today, even Adele uses the dot-dot-dot when teasing the first few chords of her new album in TV ads.

No joke, Dr. Toner even wrote a whole book about the ellipsis called *Ellipsis in English Literature: Signs of Omission* and in it she wrote that the ellipsis was "a brilliant innovation. There is no play printed before . . . that marks unfinished sentences this way."

Unfinished sentences?

What else is an unfinished sentence?

The answer is everything.

Everything you do, every path you take, every diagnosis you get, every wall you hit, every setback, every failure, every rejection. All of these experiences are part of the unfinished sentence of your life story.

Sometimes the best thing you can do is learn to add that dot-dot-dot . . . and keep going.

2

What happens when you see past the period?

et's get back to Kenya.

In my mom's case, there were massive political, cultural, and family pressures all around her, so she kept her mouth shut and her head down rather than rail against cultural norms. She added a dot-dot-dot by finding a way to keep going. She didn't shave her head and start smoking by the train tracks. No, while her three older brothers received the bulk of the family's praise, attention, and money for education, she joined her sisters sweeping floors, working the stove, and scrubbing the work clothes clean.

To keep her mind challenged, she sat on her front porch and memorized the license plates of cars driving by. She was craving a mental challenge. So she found a safe space where she could satisfy it silently.

Why license plates? "There was nothing else to memorize," she told me later. "It was a game for myself. Just to see if I could do it." She'd see a familiar car and guess the numbers from a distance, quietly congratulating herself when she got one right. At night, in the corner of the clattery kitchen, she'd study math under dim lights and curious gazes. None of her sisters worked so hard on schoolwork. Who needed to study so much just to cook curried lentils and serve chai?

Given she had seven older siblings all growing up and out of the house, the majority of her education was self-taught. Her parents didn't have time for picture books before bed or late nights patching together a volcano for the school science fair. That would have been laughable. No, it was pile of text-books, pile of paper, pile of pencils. Fend for yourself. Rinse and repeat.

All of her studying came to a head in 1963 when she took the government's standard National Exam with every other thirteen-year-old in the country.

And what happened?

She got the highest mark.

In the country!

Suddenly a fat scholarship dropped into her lap and she was whisked away from her family home to a preppy English boarding school in the countryside with all the white British kids of the colonialists. She was the youngest of eight kids and the first one to leave home for boarding school. Nevermind on a scholarship.

She added a dot-dot-dot to her story throughout her upbringing. Memorizing license plates. Extra homework. Always after cooking and cleaning.

And then?

She got past the period. Her story continued . . .

But there are always more periods up ahead.

There always are.

"I couldn't believe it," my mom told me. "The school was a heaven on Earth. The grounds were so beautiful. We knew there were schools just for white people. For the rulers. But when I got there, everybody was so rich, coming in the best cars with chauffeurs. I was overwhelmed. I was scared. I never imagined I would be allowed to go in. I didn't feel like I was equal to the other students. I just wanted to go home."

How many times have you gotten past a period and then just wanted to go home?

"I never imagined I would be allowed to go in. I didn't feel like I was equal to the other students."

How many times have you felt this way? I feel this way all the time. Finally get the promotion? Now it's new job, new boss, new way of doing things—and here comes that feeling of wanting to run for the hills. Sick family member gets better? Now you really have to confront the future you said you didn't have time for. Visa gets approved? Great! Now how do you really feel about leaving your culture and aging parents behind to start all over again?

When we get past the period, the struggle starts all over again. You may dream of tapping out, stopping before you start, sticking a big period on the end of the new sentence so you don't have to keep moving, fighting, working, trying. But it's back to doing the same thing we're talking about here.

What if you add a dot-dot-dot and keep your options open instead?

There is power in moving slowly through the motions.

There is power in letting the story continue.

3

"I don't waltz ... yet."

For the next few years, my mom's life was full of reciting the
Lord's Prayer, memorizing Shakespeare passages, and eating
soft-boiled eggs in the corner of the school cafeteria. After hitting the books away from friends and family, she graduated at
seventeen and started to feel like her life was back on the rails,
like she had made it, like everything was slowly coming together.

And then the phone rang.

And it was her father.

And he asked her to come home right away.

"I'm dying," he told her. "Go make something of yourself."

He passed away within days, just as violence and political
instability were growing in East Africa. The dictator Idi Amin
was ordering all East Asians out of neighboring Uganda and fears
were growing that Kenya would be next.

My mom had added the dot-dot-dot as a kid but was now
given new tests as a teen: her father suddenly dying, her home
country unsafe, and those same heavy cultural pressures now

falling onto my grandmother to scrape together a dowry and find her a husband.

"It's great you managed to get an education ... but now we really need to marry you off."

So my mom fled to England with her mother and lived with her in London as her older siblings scattered and settled into their own married lives. And then my dad visited from Canada on summer vacation, the families introduced them, they had one date (one!) and then an arranged marriage a couple weeks (weeks!) later. Then? He moved my mom back to his home in a small, dusty suburb an hour east of Toronto, Canada.

And it suddenly felt like *another* period.

My mom's global migration happened so quickly. She landed with a thud in that dusty suburb, with no Indian people around, suddenly married to a guy she'd met twice—including at their wedding—with her parents, siblings, and friends all an ocean away.

I can't imagine how scary that must have been.

Another challenge, another wrench, another kink in the garden hose, another place where it felt like the end of a sentence.

But she kept moving, kept going, kept adding a dot-dot-dot.

When she came to Canada my mom had eaten meat only a handful of times. My dad was a teacher and started bringing her to after-school barbecues and roast beef dinners at the Rotary Club, where they'd hang out with a couple dozen white people. Indian food wasn't widely available so it was meat, meat, and more meat. And this was the suburbs in the 70s. Saying you were a vegetarian meant picking bacon bits off your Caesar salad and going home hungry. What did my mom do? She went along with the crowd.

When she came to Canada, my mom had never been ballroom dancing in her life. She'd never heard of ballroom dancing. But my dad's idea of fun was going to Club Loreley, the local German club, and waltzing her around the room. So she let herself be waltzed. I remember hearing this story growing up and jumping in.

"But you don't waltz!" I said.

And she said, "I didn't do anything Dad did. But what was I supposed to do? Sit at home? I just told myself I don't waltz . . . yet."

I would ask her how she had navigated so many hairpin turns: new country, new husband, new job, new friends, new foods, new pastimes. She always seemed to keep moving. But how could she change everything so quickly?

Was it survival?

She told me she was just keeping her options open. Adding a dot-dot-dot to the end of the sentence. Letting things happen so she could navigate forward from a position of strength rather than feeling like all her doors had closed.

4

Keep your options infinite

An MIT study confirmed the value of adding a dot-dot-dot.

Researchers Dan Ariely and Jiwoong Shin showed that the mere *possibility* of losing an option in the future increases its attractiveness to the point that people will invest money to maintain that option. As they put it in their study: "The threat of unavailability does make the heart grow fonder."

What's the point?

The point is that although it may be hard to admit it and hard to see it and certainly hard to do it, we really do subconsciously crave adding that dot-dot-dot.

Life is a journey from infinite possibilities when you're born—you can be anything, do anything, go anywhere—to zero possibilities when you die. So I'm proposing that the real game is trying to keep those options open as long as you can.

Like the farmer, we need to add a "We'll see" when life blasts us into the stratosphere or sends us screeching wildly into the ravine beside an icy road.

We need to remember and constantly work on developing the muscle of continuing to move forward and always adding a dot-dot-dot . . .

5

The single word that makes it happen

Add a dot–dot–dot.

Sounds snappy.

But how? How can we really do that? Right as we're falling, as we're feeling it, as we're looking up at the light disappearing above us, how? What is the tool we can use to try to put this theory into practice?

Well, it comes down to adding one word to our vocabularies.

It's the word I heard my mom use over and over growing up.

And the word is "yet."

"Yet" is the magic word to add to any sentence that we begin with "I can't," "I'm not," or "I don't."

Wait! Yuck! Who talks like this? Who is that negative? Well, we all do this. We do! We *declare* things about ourselves *to* ourselves. We issue proclamations!

Pitch gets rejected? "I'm not creative."

Cut from the team? "I'm not good at sports."

Bad blood test from the lab? "I don't take care of myself."

And it's not only when we're falling, either.

Our negative talk is even more insidious when we're just moving through the motions. Just walking down the path. Painting in the paint-by-numbers. Hopscotching the chalky boxes.

Why get married if you're not in love?

"I can't meet new people."

Why put yourself last as you take care of someone you love?

"I don't have any better options."

Why go to law school if you don't want to?

"I'm no good at anything else."

We talk like this. And every time we do, we're inserting periods at the ends of sentences that we might have kept going.

I use my mom's story to show how easy it would have been for her to just stop and give up, to shut off the taps. It's much harder to keep the taps on. It's harder to add a "yet" to the end of a self-judgment.

How does the magic word look in practice?

"I can't meet new people . . . yet."

"I don't have any better options . . . yet."

"I'm not good at anything else . . . yet."

"I don't waltz . . . yet."

When we gain the courage to add a "yet" to statements about ourselves, we leave our options open. Adding the word "yet" is empowering. It wedges a little question mark into the negative certainty we hold on to so fiercely in our minds. It lets us hold both ideas. The idea that we can't. And! The idea that we can.

It leaves the door open.

It adds a "To be continued . . ."

Growing up, my mom never let her story finish.

And over the years ahead she continued to face many challenges. Sudden onset mental illness. The shocking death of her closest sister. Many moments where she could have closed things off with a period. But she always added a dot-dot-dot instead.

This is the first step to building resilience as you're falling.

Resilience is being able to see that tiny little sliver of light between the door and the frame just after you hear the latch click.

Prom invite shot down? I haven't got a date . . . yet.

Passed over for promotion? I'm not a manager . . . yet.

Cholesterol way out of whack? I don't exercise . . . yet.

My mom never added a period in the brand new continent she found herself living in in her midtwenties.

"This doesn't feel like home . . . yet."

She never added a period in the arranged marriage her family ushered her into.

"I don't know this man . . . yet."

She never added a period at the boarding school where she was asked to pray to a new God in a new religion in a new language.

"I'm not confident at this school . . . yet."

She never added a period when she was born the fifth girl in a family praying for a fourth boy.

"I don't know what I'll do . . . yet."

Setbacks didn't kill her spirit.

She just saw that sliver of light.

So when you feel like you're falling, don't just end the sentence.

Add a dot-dot-dot instead . . .

ADD A DOT-DOT-DOT

SECRET #2

Shift the Spotlight

W hat was your first full-time job?

I had a lot of part-time jobs.

Paper boy. Leaf raker. Babysitter. Pill counter at my cousin's pharmacy. I nailed those jobs! I mastered the art of flinging rubber-banded papers onto porches, raking leaves into giant piles, and playing with the kids down the street while eating all their Cheese Strings.

But my first full-time job?

Well, I was hired as Assistant Brand Manager for Covergirl and Max Factor inside the consumer packaged goods supergiant Procter & Gamble.

Or P&G as everyone called it.

It was my first job after graduating from university.

And I completely failed at it.

I took a bus and two trains to the office on my first day. I remember being twenty-two years old and walking from the subway station while staring at the opulent white P&G monolith puncturing the cloudscape, perfectly poised at the top of a long hill, shadowing down onto the busy highway and beyond.

I was a newly minted graduate filled with fear, excitement, and nervous energy, but I also had some swagger. P&G had put me and thousands of other applicants through a Math and English test, long online application, big group dinner with recruiters, first-round panel interview, and then an *American Idol*–like field trip to the big city. No, I didn't cry happy tears into the mirror with my mom while tying a plaid bandanna around my head, but the company did pay for a first-class train ticket, wine and dine me, and then place me onstage in front of a panel of judges for a grilling interview.

So why the swagger?

Because when I was hired, the recruiters told me, "We visited a dozen campuses, did a ton of interviews, brought a group of people to our head office, and we hired . . . you. You're the *only* full-time graduate we hired this year who hasn't worked here as a summer intern before."

Why me? I wondered. I was sort of average. At school many students had been far above me on the dean's list and graduated with honors. Not me. I had never hit any academic home runs. I was the guy treading water in class.

But P&G saw it differently. "See, we're looking for *well-rounded* students, not just superbrains. Our hiring process is so thorough, we weed out everyone. Well, *almost* everyone."

I did some quick math and realized that P&G had dropped well over six figures just getting me in the door. And I'd seen salary pages my school released showing how much money my fellow grads and I were getting paid. Marketing graduates received salaries from $24,000 to $51,000.

And my starting salary was $51,000. That meant I was the highest-paid marketing graduate in my year! I was at the top of the entire salary range.

And that didn't include the signing bonus, four weeks vacation, and more benefits than I could ever use.

Benefits? What benefits?

Crazy benefits.

I'm talking about two *ergonomists* in white smocks visiting my desk to make sure all my heating and cooling vents were properly aimed, my desk and keyboard were in the correct position, and the tilted footrest beneath my cheap dress shoes was inclined at some proper ergonomic angle. I was shown a button I could press on my phone that dialed a P&G department *in Costa Rica* so that I could change the temperature at my desk anytime I wanted. Braces? Counseling? Shoe insoles? All covered! I was even given a couple thousand dollars a year to spend on massages with the three full-time massage therapists *working right inside the office* every single day. "Please," they were saying, "let's rub out that knotty, knotty back of yours between meetings whenever we can."

I walked into the P&G lobby on my first day feeling like I was Charlie Bucket holding the golden ticket.

I met my boss Stacey in the lobby. She was half an hour late and apologized as we took the elevator up to my new desk. We walked out of the elevator into a cubicle-walled jigsaw puzzle that felt like one of those boxes they make white mice run through to find the cheese. Men with furrowed brows wearing crisp dress shirts and holding stacks of paper from the photocopier *actually ran past me.* Glass walls on all sides of the floor flashed a picture-perfect postcard view of luscious green valleys, mighty down-town skyscrapers, and the shimmering blue lake beyond.

I was shown my desk, which was outfitted with a laptop locked to a docking station. Stacey saw me staring at the lock. "Don't worry," she said, "we shackle the computer to the desk, not your ankles. Espionage and headhunters are big in this in-dustry. Competitors have gone through our dumpsters. We take confidentiality seriously."

She handed me a box of business cards that, to emphasize the point, simply had my name, the name of the company, and the general phone number.

No job title, no email address, no direct phone line, nothing.

I felt like an assassin.

"We don't put your job title or contact information on your business cards because headhunters map our org charts. And if your direct contact information appeared on the cards, you'd be getting calls all day. Everybody knows working at P&G is *the* ticket to any marketing job in the world. Our receptionists are trained to weed out headhunters and competitors, so you won't be bothered while you're working."

The joke I'd heard about becoming a "Proctoid" was start-ing to make sense. When I told older friends I was working at Procter & Gamble, they described Procter employees as these beautiful, hypersuccessful androids who smiled with perfect teeth, were always nice in meetings, worked out at the gym, ate super-healthy, spoke and wrote the same way, and even wore the same kinds of clothes.

Proctoids.

Next up on my first day was "Breakfast with the President." I sat with the president of the company and all the people returning to full-time roles from their summer internships. As we went around the table sharing our backgrounds, I realized I was the only total newbie.

Then it was time for the president to speak to us. He was a polished, good-looking guy in his late forties with a thick, wavy black mane.

"You'll notice everyone in this room is a fresh graduate from a top business school," he began. "That's all we hire. We have a hundred percent promote-from-within policy. We don't hire people with two years of experience, five years of experience, or ten years of experience. We only hire people with zero years of experience.

"We want you to be successful here. In fact, we *need* you to be successful. If you fail, it means there's an air bubble in our promotion system. So here's the way it works. Half of you will be promoted to the next level in two to three years. Half of those folks will go to the level after that. Half of *those* will go to the level after that. And so on. Twenty years ago, I started in the same seat you're in now."

The guy was impressive. We all wanted to be like him.

It was clear we were young, fresh, and moldable.

It was clear this was a real Charlie Bucket opportunity.

What wasn't clear was that I was about to fall on my face.

★ ★ ★

Once I finished all the introductory meetings and email-writing workshops, I finally started to get my bearings.

Although it didn't say it on my business card, my job title was Assistant Brand Manager for Covergirl and Max Factor makeup. I was responsible for the entire Max Factor brand, which was fairly small, and the gigantic Eyes and Lips category of Covergirl.

Eyes and Lips!

It sounds like I was a third-rate butcher in a rough part of town.

So what does an Assistant Brand Manager do? Well, I was the boss of the brand. I got to decide where to advertise, how much to advertise, what every product should cost, when to introduce a new product, and when to take one away.

How was I supposed to do that?

By pulling data from a ton of different sources, dropping it into gigantic Excel spreadsheets, and then creating graphs and charts that ended up as bullet points in famous internal P&G documents known as one-page recos.

Maybe I wanted to recommend ditching all our print ads in favor of more online ads. I'd spend two weeks finding all the historical sales data mapped against all print and online ad campaigns and make statistical extrapolations to prove that every dollar in online ads resulted in three dollars in sales versus every dollar in print resulting in two dollars in sales. I'd then drop all my findings into a one-page reco and spend another two weeks presenting it in meetings until I got all the big bosses to sign off on it.

To get all that done, I stayed at work until 10:00 p.m. And I did reconnaissance, just like an assassin. With my coworker Ben, we visited the pharmacy next door, secretly wrote down the prices of all the products on the shelves, then came back and typed them into Excel spreadsheets.

"You have to do this for every single retailer across the country," Ben said.

"How long will that take?"

"Maybe two weeks," he said, "if you do it every night. You may have to drive a long way or call people in different cities. You also have to pull all the costs and historical costs for every single item from this archaic data system, which is really confusing and often doesn't include all the data you need."

I thought marketing would be a PowerPoint job.

Graphics, pictures, ideas.

But it was an Excel job.

Collecting data, writing formulas, crunching numbers.

Not long into my tenure, my eyes got crossed staring at the screen all day. I could never pull the data properly. I sucked at finding errors in five-hundred-row spreadsheets, and the requests in my inbox piled up at triple the speed I was able to answer them, which left me in a constant state of anxiety and helplessness.

My negative self-talk amped up. It was all about me. Every sentence started with "I suck," "I'm not able," or "I can't." We don't notice how naturally such self-stabbing moments come when we're starting to fall.

It wasn't long before things got even worse.

I went to a meeting with Tony, my boss's boss, where he

quizzed me about some elements of the upcoming Covergirl Outlast lipstick launch I was fuzzy on.

I got a scolding from Stacey after the meeting.

"I expect you to know all your numbers!" she warned.

"But there are fifteen hundred items and I have no idea what he's going to ask. It's too much to memorize."

She shot me an angry look. I started working evenings and weekends. I felt I was the problem. Clearly I wasn't working hard enough. This is the equivalent of thrashing your arms and legs to go faster in the pool.

When I went to work on weekends, I was surprised to find the office parking lot full of sports cars while we crunched Excel spreadsheets upstairs trying to figure out where to advertise the new deodorant or whether we should discontinue one-ply toilet paper in favor of three-ply toilet paper.

It felt like a problem of time.

It felt like a problem of me.

For those who have felt it before, you know there is a deep, pit-of-the-stomach sensation when you go to work feeling like you simply aren't good at your job. That's the part we often miss when we see people who aren't pulling their weight. We miss the fact that *they don't like it either.*

Nobody wakes up wanting to be terrible at their job.

It feels awful when you're bad and you know it.

It's different from feeling like you're new and learning. It's different from feeling like you aren't being treated fairly or the system is out to get you.

What I'm talking about is walking into your workplace on

a Monday morning feeling like a failure. Feeling like the exact thing you're supposed to do is something you desperately want to be able to do and would put anything into doing it well, but it just feels like you'll never get there.

We fill our minds with inspirational messages encouraging us to "Just do it!" or "Follow your heart!" so when we can't do something or we recognize we aren't good at something, we feel stuck. If we quit, that's a problem ("Just do it! *Don't give up!*"), and if we stick with it, that's also a problem ("Follow your heart! *Do what you love!*").

As a result the self-help industry can actually be pretty toxic and offer a surprising amount of contradictory advice. Contradictions don't do us much good when we're suffering from a Han Solo frozen-in-carbonite feeling.

Arms up, mouth open, eyebrows pained.

Unable to move at all.

I started grinding my teeth, tossing and turning at night, and waking up with a feeling of dread in my stomach.

I was starting to mentally cast a play called *Death of a Cubicle Worker*. I put myself in the lead role in the center of the stage, staring at the audience with my saucer-like eyes as the red velvet curtain rolled up.

And then a spotlight started shining.

On my eyes.

On my face.

On my failure.

1

Who fails hardest and what can we do about it?

The psychology researcher Marisen Mwale at the Msuzu University in Malawi did a study that looked at the perceived causes of failure between low- and high-achieving adolescents.

Like many good studies, it confirmed what most of us already suspected: everybody fails. We know that. But what happens when *high achievers* fail? You guessed it. They fail harder, much harder, than low achievers do.

"It's on me," they think. "I failed because even though I tried really hard, I wasn't good enough." Or "I failed because *I'm* the problem."

What about low achievers? They more often blame their failures on bad luck or the difficulty of the task. Sure, maybe they whine more, but they are also more likely to honestly recognize when the system doesn't allow for their success. They are easier on themselves. They admit that factors beyond their control may have affected the outcome.

As stakes continuously rise, as standards endlessly elevate, as the pinch of performance gets even tighter, there's a real risk that more of us will be in this high-achieving, hard-on-ourselves category. Maybe you already are? I know I am.

So what can we do about it?

Well, one thing we can do is this: we can talk about it more, share our failures, ask for help, and scrub the sheen of perfection right off of us.

Why? What's that going to do?

Well, Karen Huang, Alison Wood Brooks, Ryan W. Buell, Brian Hall, and Laura Huang at Harvard Business School published a working paper called "Mitigating Malicious Envy: Why Successful Individuals Should Reveal Their Failures." Their study found that discussing failures helps humanize us. Of course it does!

When I tell you, "Oh man, I screwed up," I seem normal, real, and relatable. Then what happens? Well, interpersonal relationships improve when we empathize with each other's failures. And you know what else? This is the fun part: levels of "benign envy" actually increase in others.

What's benign envy?

It's the good kind of envy. The opposite of malicious envy. Benign envy actually motivates others, lets people see you as a role model. Benign envy is contagious in a good way. It motivates others to improve their own performance.

So next time you screw up and feel like hiding it, remember you're doing no one any good that way. So share, fess up, let others in, because then others will empathize with you and keep growing.

2

You think you don't fit but you do

What was happening at P&G?

What was really going on during this spiral?

The issue was I was telling myself it was all about me.

I was taking my performance, results, and feedback and projecting it back onto the movie screen of my mind with big, ugly phrases like "I suck at my job" and "I'm failing my bosses" and "I'm losing the company money."

Remember the high-achiever study?

I was blaming myself for everything. I was telling myself it was all about me.

The problem is that when we make such self-harming projections, we believe them.

Our minds are so sharp they can shatter us.

To show how dangerous this is, let's look at a 2013 study called "Too Fat to Fit Through the Door" by Anouk Keizer and a team of researchers from Utrecht University in the Netherlands.

The researchers watched women with anorexia and women without anorexia walk through doorways while asking them to do a simple task that mentally distracted them from paying attention to their bodies.

What happened?

Anorexics turned their shoulders and squeezed sideways through the doorways much more than the group without anorexia did. Even though they had plenty of room to walk right through, they thought they were too fat to fit.

Am I saying you have anorexia? Am I saying you have an eating disorder? Am I saying you have a mental illness? No, no, no, none of that. So what am I saying, then?

Your image of yourself may be projecting outward in your actions in potentially nonsensical ways.

Especially if you're hard on yourself like I am.

What doorways are you trying to squeeze yourself through right now where . . . you know what?

You really fit just fine. You probably aren't the problem.

And what about our modern environment?

Does it help prevent us from separating ourselves from the challenges we face? Does it make us believe it's all our fault?

Yes, yes, definitely yes.

We live in a world where the screws are on tight. There's a capitalistic shrink wrap making sure everything is fitter, happier, and more productive. So sometimes the stress on all of us builds too high.

See, nobody at P&G ever said to me, "This is gonna take a while, Neil" or "It's normal to feel like you don't know anything for six months" or "Let's get a few flops out of your system so you can learn how to do it."

No, nobody was that lax. They couldn't afford to be! Our world no longer has space to be lax. We no longer have space to be patient with you, to slowly train you, to let you make little failures and learn from them. We're running our races so fast that we need to pass the baton to a supertrained all-star on Day 1 every time!

Now, that doesn't mean my bosses at P&G were cruel. They absolutely weren't. My point is that they had lofty expectations and needed me to help. Fast! The screws were tight on them, too.

No wonder it's such a hard lesson to learn as we're falling that we're okay, we're okay, we're okay. And maybe it's just not about us. It's not about us. It's not about us. Why is it hard to learn? Because nobody else is telling us that! Not the messages online, not the world we live in, not our bosses at work. So we think it's always all about us. When we fail we dig the point of a knife into our stomach and give it a twist.

What are we doing to ourselves?

Well, a study published in *Psychological Bulletin* in 2016 declared that "Perfectionism Is Increasing over Time." In the study, researchers Thomas Curran of the University of Bath and Andrew P. Hill of York St John University claim that "recent generations of young people perceive that others are more demanding of them, are more demanding of others, and are more demanding of themselves."

We want to be perfect so badly.

Which makes our flops hurt even more.

3

Don't magnify. Don't biggify. Don't amplify.

Within a couple more months at P&G, I was placed on a Performance Improvement Plan, also known as a PIP. This is an elaborate document essentially saying "We want to fire you, but we don't have enough of a paper trail, so let's build one together!"

I responded poorly to being PIPed. I was angry, feisty, and pouty about the whole thing. I acted in ways I regret, like speaking poorly about my boss, becoming snippy in email exchanges, and exchanging dramatic quitting scenarios with friends over Instant Messenger.

"Kick over all the filing cabinets," my friend Joey advised me. "Toss someone's plant through the glass window."

I see now that my anger stemmed from my deep disappointment in myself.

That was the root emotion.

I thought I sucked. And I didn't like sucking. So I lashed out. Blamed others. And that greased the wheels for my downward spiral, because now in addition to producing lame results, I became a giant pain in the ass to work with.

We have to remember that sometimes the "angry and underperforming" coworker just started out as underperforming . . . and nobody helped them.

I remember sitting in a boardroom at a different company many years after I left P&G.

A bunch of executives dug into a low-level manager about his poor monthly numbers. After the grillfest finished and the underperforming manager left on the verge of tears, the CEO said something from the corner of the room that I'll never forget. He shook his head a little. But not at the underperforming manager. At his executive team who had just torn a strip off the poor sap. The room was quiet and he just said a couple of profound sentences.

He said: "He doesn't need to know he's doing it wrong. He needs to know how to do it right."

And that's the root of it.

At P&G, things only got worse. I used company benefits to get outfitted for a mouth guard because I was so anxious I had started grinding my teeth in my sleep. I kept working evenings and weekends hoping a light would go off and I'd suddenly become a whiz at crunching numbers and keeping up with email. My boss would ping me with subject lines that read "Hi Neil— Quick five-minute request!—Response requested," and then I'd spend three days trying to come up with the analysis to answer her request and watch as she documented my performance in the Performance Improvement Plan.

"Took three days to do five-minute request."

I was getting lost in how bad I was at everything and started mentally extrapolating from those pains. I felt like my team members and my bosses and the company were all staring at me through disappointed, tear-filled eyes, watching my expensive and fancy career fly off the cliff and explode into a huge ball of flames.

I told myself that if everyone knew I was bad at this job, then marketing was out as a career option for me. My next potential employer would call my bosses at P&G who would tell them I sucked. And I told myself since marketing was my best class at school nothing else was even an option. I told myself I couldn't handle another office job and if I left an office job I was also leaving a place to meet my future wife, because offices are places full of other educated young professionals.

I would have no community. There would be no people like me. Anywhere. Period.

I pictured being fifty-five years old, greasing my hair back, selling refurbished VCRs at a trade show in Cleveland while desperately hitting on awkward salespeople at the hotel bar before striking out and pathetically masturbating all alone on top of scratchy white sheets, surrounded by metal room service trays of cold leftover club sandwiches and fries in front of an old TV playing reruns of *ALF.*

When things don't go our way, we exaggerate the size of our problems. We biggify them! We catastrophize! We see the door as too small to fit through. We feel everyone's eyes on our ineptitude. We decide the nightmare is only going to get worse!

But what if we're wrong?

4

The spotlight effect

Back in 2000, a strange term made its way into the world of psychology by way of the journal *Current Directions in Psychological Science*. The psychologists Thomas Gilovich and Kenneth Savitsky coined the term "spotlight effect."

What's the spotlight effect?

It's the feeling that we're being noticed, watched, observed, and, importantly, *judged* much more than we really are. Because we are the centers of our own worlds, we believe we're the center of everyone else's world, too.

Gilovich, at Cornell University, teamed up with Justin Kruger at the University of Illinois at Urbana-Champaign and Victoria Medvec at Northwestern University to look deeper into the spotlight effect. They took a group of Cornell students and asked them to estimate their abilities in the eyes of others in three areas: physical appearance, athletic accomplishment, and how well they played a video game.

Guess what? The participants constantly overestimated the extent to which their strengths and weaknesses would be noted by observers. Was that a big deal? Yes! The researchers said that fear of judgment can contribute to social anxiety and gnawing regrets.

So if we think the spotlight is always on us, but it isn't, what's the takeaway?

It's simple.

Shift the spotlight.

Remember you're under the belief the spotlight is shining on you and everyone in the darkened audience is staring and watching and waiting.

But they're not.

So how can you mentally shift the spotlight away from the focus on yourself?

Tim Urban writes the incredibly popular blog *Wait But Why*, and one of his most widely shared posts is "Taming the Mammoth: Why You Should Stop Caring What Other People Think." The post alone is worth the read, but he also adds two cartoons near the end that made me laugh out loud in recognition of what we're talking about here.

The first cartoon shows *how we think things are*.

It features you as a stick figure surrounded by a huge mob of people all staring at you. This is how we think things are! It's the spotlight effect. The caption says, "Everyone is talking about me and my life and just think about how much everyone will be talking about it if I do this risky or weird thing."

The second cartoon shows *how things actually are.*

And how are things actually?

Like this:

The caption below the second cartoon says, "No one really cares that much about what you're doing. People are highly self-absorbed."

We believe there's a spotlight on us.

But there isn't.

When we fail, we think all eyes are on us. We think it's all about us! Sucking at a job means being publicly humiliated and sleeping with a tray of club sandwiches or living in a box on the street. A bad breakup means no more relationships ever. One rejected college application means you're clearly an airhead whose life is about to get stuck in a world of grueling, minimum-wage pain.

We take tiny strings of trouble and extrapolate them into huge problems with our entire identities always on the line.

And the younger we are, the more we do this since we have less experience to help us understand that things usually work out okay in the end. Once you get through one tough breakup, you're a little better on the next one. Once you get through three, you're a lot better. Once you suck at one job, you're a little stronger the next time.

But that first failure really is terrible.

5

How do you shift the spotlight?

I quit Procter & Gamble.

I did it in an attempt to save a little bit of face.

As my Performance Improvement Plan kept filling up, I knew I was about to get turfed in a few weeks. But I couldn't emotionally handle the idea that I was going to be fired. So I gave the company what I thought it wanted . . . and I quit.

After getting through all the fiery hiring hoops and scoring the big salary and letting my confidence float up up up, I quit my dream job at the superstar company. I said goodbye to my great paycheck, goodbye to massages, goodbye to working with people my own age, goodbye to a snazzy corporate identity. I threw it all away and felt sick and horrible and disappointed and embarrassed and ashamed of myself.

Like I said: *that first failure really does hurt.*

I didn't see then and I wouldn't see for at least ten years that the P&G failure helped me get more comfortable with being uncomfortable. It helped me discover the feeling of performing poorly and learn to *dance with it*, to sidestep it, to have it beside me but not *inside me* forever.

How do we shift the spotlight?

We have to be aware and remember that we are quick to internalize. To self-flagellate. To point the dagger straight at our stomachs. To let the spotlight shine brightly into our own set of eyes. But a big part of resilience, of remembering we really are awesome, is performing this crucial mental separation.

"Oh, wait. I'm thinking this failure is all about me. I'm pointing the spotlight at myself. I'm taking all the blame here."

Stop. Separate. Remember:

It's actually egotistical to think it's all about you.

Position it that way in your mind. Why? Because it's true. Consider how many other factors are involved! Consider how many factors are far beyond your control.

Did you get dinged on the college application you were counting on? Well, sure, you can beat yourself up. Blind yourself with the spotlight! Or you can remember that the college had a ton of good applicants. Numbers. Quotas. Beds. It has admissions agents who are human and who may have bad days or unconscious biases or maybe know more than you do about whether or not you'd really be a good fit.

It's egotistical, arrogant, conceited to think it's all about you.

Shift that spotlight from yourself by remembering it's not always about you and remembering it's arrogant to always think it is.

So what do you do?

Dance with it. Work with it.

Set it beside you, not inside you.

It's not about you. It's not about you. It's not about you.

You have to shift that spotlight.

Why?

Because there's a lot more work to do.

And you can't start till after you shift that light.

ADD A DOT-DOT-DOT

◇

SHIFT THE SPOTLIGHT

SECRET #3

See It as a Step

I met her at a Pixies concert.

I was twenty-four years old and we were with mutual friends all shuffling and singing along at the back of a warehouse near the airport on a warm fall night.

"This is my favorite song!" she screamed over guitars wailing "Wave of Mutilation." "From *Pump Up the Volume* when I was a kid!"

A couple loud parties later, we broke off on our own and had those slow and dreamy dates with long conversations, deep knowing smiles, and telling waitress after waitress, "Sorry, we haven't even looked at the menu yet."

She ate ice cream for breakfast and gourmet pasta for dinner. An old soul with old values, she was completely at ease with herself, just as comfortable eating cold pizza off a paper towel as dressing to the nines to hobnob at a fancy holiday party.

Confident and strong as an ox, she was a natural athlete who played on the eighth grade basketball team when she was in fifth grade. Shuttled from practice to practice from team to team, she learned to be a team player, lose with grace, and eat dinner in the car.

She had wanted to be a teacher since she was ten years old.

After getting her teaching degree, she joined the public school system, and since every student at her school suffered from a learning disability, she spent hours mastering The Hygiene Conversation, The Protection Conversation, and The What the Hell Do I Do After High School Conversation.

A ring of keys jingling around her neck, plum-sized bruises on her thighs, she'd come home sweaty and sunburned after a volleyball game and spend evenings preparing math lessons, baking cookies for birthdays, or just going out to see "her kids," as she called them, play baseball with their city teams on local diamonds.

Fresh love fuels you like a drug and gives you energy you didn't know you had. After I left P&G, I didn't know what to do, so I started a sandwich restaurant with my dad in my hometown. I threw in some applications to go back to school, but I really felt I had to make a go of it. I wanted to prove to myself that I could be successful at something. Something! Anything! So after I locked up the shop at night, I would drive a couple hours through snowstorms to her apartment wearing my sticky, mustard-smeared T-shirt, smelling like cured salami and dirty dishwater but feeling on top of the world, even though I had to turn around and drive back a few hours later.

But it was always worth it.

She warmed me up with a greasy grilled cheese and we put on mittens and went for moonlit walks around the tiny lake behind her place. Blurry blotches of wet snow coming down all around us, we trudged over a slippery river bridge between tall trees and held each other's mittened hands. Noses red and sniffling, eyes alive and twinkling, we stared at each other and kissed in one of those magical movie moments.

After winter warmed into spring, after spring warmed into summer, on a less slippery bridge over a less frozen river . . . I proposed.

And she said yes.

Meanwhile, my restaurant had been sputtering.

Some months I made money. Some months I didn't. I spent too many Friday nights scrubbing toilets and burning brain cells with foamy oven cleaner. I felt like a failure all over again. I was having trouble zooming out of my struggles and shifting the spotlight away from myself.

When a letter arrived saying I somehow got into Harvard, it felt like a dolphin coming to rescue me in the middle of the ocean. I grabbed onto its fin, sold my restaurant, and let it jump me through the waves to Boston to go back to school.

We got webcams, long-distance plans, and frequent flyer cards to see each other over every long weekend and holiday. We spent the year planning our wedding and the next summer tied the knot under high blue skies on a sunny day in July.

And then I left for my second year of school.

This time she came with me and tried to get a transfer to teach in a Boston high school, but never-ending paperwork problems left her handing out towels at the Harvard gym rather than finding a local batch of kids to teach and coach. She badly missed teaching and by Christmas we agreed she'd go home and I'd follow with my degree a few months later in the spring.

And when that next winter warmed into spring and I sat in a cap and gown in front of a stage in Harvard Yard listening to the commencement speaker, I couldn't stop smiling. Because it really felt like I was finally finally *finally* getting my life together and my wife and I were going to truly start our lives together.

I moved home, I moved in, we bought a couch, we bought a house, we painted walls, we barbecued burgers, and we tried settling into the long, happy life we had first begun picturing on those slow dreamy dates three years earlier.

And even though we really, really wanted our marriage to work, sometimes heaven just doesn't last.

I remember when I knew.

There was a summer day we spent climbing a small mountain in the Adirondacks. She had been gung ho all day, on her hands and knees, scrambling up giant flattened rocks, excited to stare into the tree-lined horizon at every new lookout. I was always fifty steps behind, groaning about how tired and sore I was. She was thrilled with the adventure itself and loved the fresh air and sights and smells of nature. I was missing the four-hour conversation I was expecting and spent my time swatting mosquitos, scraping my knees, and worrying I heard bears behind me.

When we finally collapsed in our hotel room that night, there was silence between us. I could feel something. I guess she could, too. Despite being together all day we hadn't spoken much at all.

"How do you feel things are going . . . with us?" I asked softly, quietly, a bit boldly.

I wanted her to pull the anxiety out of my stomach. To tell me everything was okay. To let me slam shut the little door I was opening in my brain. To help me out of the swirling sea in my mind that was telling me to brace myself for another big failure.

But she didn't.

"I think . . . we're pretty different," she said.

"Well," I said, "they say opposites attract."

"Yeah, it's just . . ." Her voice trailed off.

"What is it?"

"You proposed so quickly and moved to Boston for two years for school. Maybe we're only getting to know each other now."

Neither one of us said anything else that night.

A few months later, the conversation continued. I got home from work one night to find her waiting outside the front door. I watched as she summoned up a lot of courage, through a lot of tears, to finally say, "Neil, I don't know if I'm in love with you anymore."

"I think we should get a divorce."

Her words were full of compassion and empathy and heartache, but they still sent me reeling.

I suddenly felt everything around me falling away. My marriage, my home, my future kids. The failures around my first job and my bumbling restaurant that I'd thought were scabbed over were suddenly raw and searing again, too.

The life I thought I was living crumbled in seconds.

And I was in shock.

I was flailing, I was falling.

What do you do when you're falling?

What are you supposed to do?

The first step is to **add a dot-dot-dot**.

That means finding the strength to keep going. Hanging in there. Continuing to breathe. Keep your heart beating. Keep moving. Even a little. Add a little dot-dot-dot, add a "yet" to your thoughts, and take it day by day or moment by moment.

The second step is to **shift the spotlight**.

That's harder, sure, but necessary. Vital. It means separating your version of the story from *the* story. Remember, we tend to shine a spotlight on ourselves as though we're the center of everything. We make everything about us. But instead, we need to learn to dance with it, to place it beside us, not inside us.

And the third step?

The third step is to **see it as a step**.

To see the failure you're going through as a step up an invisible staircase toward a Future You in a Future Life you can't even imagine yet.

This is hard. Really hard! It has to do with trusting the process, trusting yourself, knowing you've been okay before, and believing that after losses and setbacks, things often get back on track.

But if you can't see the rest of the invisible staircase, how do you trust it's there?

1

The end of history illusion

H ere's the thing. The staircase represents your life so far.

And you can't see up the invisible staircase.

Look down behind you! That part is visible. You can see where you came from. All the steps you already walked up. Oh, look! There's the time you moved in fifth grade and got bullied by that goon Adam every day after school. Remember? That's when you first picked up a basketball and started practicing with Coach Williams every night. There's Francesco, the tattooed chef who chewed you out every shift you showed up late to wash dishes at the seafood place as a teen. It was painful but you learned to be on time and still go back for his famous crab cakes when you're in town. Oh! Prom! Yikes! Remember that disaster? I guess that night helped you realize you were gay. Thank goodness your parents were so loving and supportive when you came out before going off to college. What a relief.

So many steps up to today. Big steps. Hard steps. But steps all the same.

And what's next on the staircase?

Well, that's the problem.

No one knows.

It's invisible.

We can't see the future.

And maybe if that were the only problem, that would be okay.

But it isn't. It gets worse.

Why?

Because according to the research, we actually think we *can* see up that staircase!

Our brains think, "Oh yeah, sure, I know what's next in my life." We imagine those stairs and we think we're good at imagining them! But in reality, we suck at it.

Let me explain.

Back in January 2013, *Science* magazine published a fascinating study conducted by the researchers Jordi Quoidbach, Daniel T. Gilbert, and Timothy D. Wilson. They teamed up to measure the personalities, values, and preferences of more than 19,000 people aged 18 to 68. Through a series of tests, they asked the subjects about two pretty simple things: how much they thought they had changed in the past decade and how much they would change in the next decade.

They used a lot of fancy scientific methods to make sure the data were legit. Then they published their results.

What happened?

Academic circles started buzzing.

Media outlets clamored to share the results.

Why?

Because the results were mind blowing! It turned out that no matter how old the respondents were they uniformly believed that they had changed a ton in the past but would change little in the future.

What?

So imagine a 30-year-old guy telling the tempestuous story of his last ten years but figuring his next ten years would be smooth sailing. Imagine a 50-year-old woman talking about how everything had flip-flopped after she turned 40 but then assuming that at 60, she'd be the same person she was now. That was the case for everybody regardless of age, gender, or personality. We all do it!

We all think that the way things are *now* is the way things will continue to be.

If you're flying high, that's maybe not a bad thing, but if you're falling, if you're broken, if you're busted, if you're heartbroken, if you're lonely, then this is a dangerous psychological tendency. And we all share it.

When we're at rock bottom, we are certain that there's no way up. We think we'll never get out of our parents' basement. We think our divorce means we'll never meet someone new. We think if we've lost our jobs we'll be scrolling online temp postings forever.

The researchers called this the "end of history illusion."

We think all our wild stories stop exactly now and everything will remain unchanged from here on out.

Now: Why did those researchers spend so long studying 19,000 people?

Daniel Gilbert, one of the researchers, went on NPR's *Hidden Brain* and explained, "You know, like everybody, I suffer the slings and arrows of outrageous fortune. You know, we have divorces. We have surgeries. We have breakups with women we love and friends we enjoy. So it was sort of ordinary events that befell me all in one year. And I realized that, had you asked me a year earlier how I would be faring, the answer would have been, oh, my gosh, I'll be devastated. But I wasn't devastated. . . . And it made me wonder if I was the only person who was just too stupid to be able to look ahead into his future and figure out how he'd feel if really bad or maybe really good things happened."

Aha! There it is. The invisible staircase.

Even Daniel Gilbert, *the* Daniel Gilbert, the famed Harvard psychologist and professor, the author of bestselling books such as *Stumbling on Happiness*, even *he* forgets that the rest of the staircase is invisible. He went through a flop or two and figured, "Well, darn, my life's gonna suck forever." But it didn't. Because inevitably everything we go through in life *really is a step to help us get to a better place.*

It's hard to see it this way. It's so hard to see it this way! But we have to, we have to, because this left brain–scratching study helps us realize we're prone to catastrophizing. And that alone should be enough to zoom backward in your brain and go "Wait a minute here. I'm tricking myself! Maybe everything won't be awful forever! Who's to say I won't get out of the basement? Meet someone new? Land a plum gig I love?"

See it as a step.

Dan Gilbert ended up figuring out that when it comes to predicting the future, we're all stupid. Each and every one of us.

How relieving! See, you're not stupid. *We're* stupid. You're not an idiot. *We're* idiots. You're not dumb. *We're all dumb.*

Doesn't that feel better?

This research reminded me of an HR job I had where I had to escort bosses into meeting rooms whenever they had to fire an employee. I was there for paperwork, I was there for witnessing, I was there for emotional support. I was in the room when dozens of people got fired and it was awful. There were tears and wet tissues and many afternoons when I'd be consoling someone in a freezing parking lot as they loaded up their trunk with framed pictures from their desk saying "I thought I'd be here forever" and "What am I going to do now?" and "I'll never find another job."

Those scenes left me heartbroken.

I lost a lot of sleep over them.

But sometimes I'd bump into the former employees again years later. And what did they tell me? Every single time? "Getting fired was the best thing that happened to me! If I hadn't gotten that severance package, I never would have had those crucial six months to spend with my dad before he died."

Or: "I traveled to Peru and became a nutritional supplement importer, and I love what I'm doing now!"

Or: "I'm working at a smaller company now, and I've gotten promoted twice in two years!"

Or: "I used my severance pay to take the time to be with my daughter and son-in-law in the months after her third miscarriage."

Why did every fired employee tell me this? Why did they

all react so positively after some time had passed? How can that happen?

Because we confuse the challenge of picturing change with the improbability of change itself.

We do.

We confuse the challenge of picturing change ("What am I going to do now?") with the improbability of change ("I'll never find anything!").

In other words, you can't *picture* yourself changing so you assume you won't.

Why?

Because your seeing skills are shit!

And so are mine. So are everyone's.

You think because you can't see up the staircase there aren't any more steps.

But there *are* more steps.

And change will come.

It always does.

That's why it's so hard to see change as a step. To see this failure, this flop, this difficult life experience as part of a process, as part of a greater whole. It's hard to see it as a step because you can't see the next step! And you sure can't see ten steps after that.

Why do we always think failure leads somewhere bad? It's not true. It rarely is. Remember the end of history illusion. Our brains think this is the end! Remember all those people I met after they were fired saying how positive that jarring left turn ended up being in their lives? It's me, too. How could I have known that failing at P&G would somehow lead us to having the conversation we're having right now? I couldn't have. Believe me, I far prefer having this conversation to doing price analysis on eye shadows and mascaras. But when I flamed out there I pictured myself sleeping in a pile of club sandwich crusts in Cleveland.

So be kind to yourself, too.

When you're there, when you're stewing in the shock of failure and loss, when you're convinced you're stuck, when you're convinced there's no way forward, just remember: there's a staircase you're not seeing. Trust that it's there, right in front of you, and that it leads to exciting new places. Have the courage to believe in this one thing that you can't see.

There are so many steps ahead. So many steps. Don't stop. Add a dot-dot-dot. Shift the spotlight and keep moving.

Sure, you're going through a failure.

But it's very possible, and very likely, that what you're going through is a step toward a future you'll be happy with. But you just can't see it . . . yet.

2

Go back to the beginning

S o.

   We did it.

   We got the divorce.

   With pits in our stomachs, with holes in our hearts, we put
the house up for sale, we met with a family lawyer, we went to
a courthouse, we processed the paperwork, we packed up our
boxes, and we stumbled through the awkwardness of splitting up
our furniture and carrying it out of our house with random people we had spent years turning into mothers- and fathers-in-laws
right as they were turning back into random people again.

   I moved into a tiny 500-square-foot bachelor apartment
downtown in a building called The Hudson. A friend helped me
move my dining room table up the elevator and we set the whole
thing up before realizing it filled the whole kitchen. So we took it
all apart and moved it back out. I never replaced the table. I never
bought kitchen chairs. I never bought bowls or oven trays or salt
and pepper shakers. My cupboards were empty.

   So was my fridge.

So was my heart.

I was embarrassed by the black bags growing under my eyes so I bought a fancy eye cream from the drugstore down the street and started applying it under my eyes every morning. I didn't want people knowing I had been up all night suffering from intense sleeplessness, anxiety, and loneliness.

For the first time in my life I was living alone, living in a big city, with every single thing I'd hoped for by the time I was 30 washed out to sea . . .

No marriage, no house, no kids.

Back to the beginning.

Most of my friends were married with kids in the suburbs and I had six contacts in my cell phone. I didn't know anyone in the neighborhood and had nothing to do and nowhere to go.

Over the months this was all happening I was angry, I was sad, I was trudging to work every day, I was sitting through meetings like a zombie, I was coming home to take-out dinners every night.

One day as I was driving home from work I told myself, "There's gotta be *something* positive out there."

A tiny little flare. A tiny brain bolt. Something to grab on to. Something to listen to. I decided I had to find it. A positive thing. I just had to turn over a new leaf! I just had to *change the channel!* So when I got home from work I turned on . . . CNN.

Do not do that.

Every single TV station, every single newspaper, every single radio station is bad news.

I'm being honest when I tell you that I don't listen to a single news channel or watch a single news show today. I have canceled all my newspaper and magazine subscriptions. I have no news sites bookmarked. I get enough from skimming headlines at the grocery store, and I willingly sacrifice *knowing deeply* what's going on in order to live a more content life. Can you imagine how many apartment building fires and traffic jam updates and reality TV star engagements we're both missing out on right now?

Now, I'm not saying you should put your fingers in your ears and scream LALALALALALALA as loud as you can when people start talking about climate change. What I'm saying is the world is full of bad news and our primal brains are desperate to read it so our media outlets are desperate to hawk it for dollars.

The solution is to be intentional about your attention.

Chop all sites out, and then choose the issues you care about, study them deeply, and act accordingly. Just stop being on the receiving end of the rat-a-tat-tat machine-gun barrage of superficial negativity fired at you from every elevator television, treadmill, and radio station.

So back then I flipped off CNN and went online. I typed, "How to start a blog" into Google and then pressed the "I'm feeling lucky" button that no one ever presses.

Ten minutes later I had started a tiny website called 1000 AwesomeThings.com as a way to try to put a smile on my face before I went to bed. The writing started off very sarcastic. Acerbic. Cynical. Reflective of the cynical way I was feeling. I wrote about how fat baseball players give us hope. I wrote about how locking people out of the car and pretending to drive away is the world's best gag. I wrote and I wrote and I wrote.

Every day I'd come home from work and add another one. What about putting on warm underwear just out of the dryer? Or flipping to the cold side of the pillow in the middle of the night? Hitting a string of green lights when you're late for work? Finally peeing after holding it forever?

The writing was cathartic. It was a release. It helped me swap dark thoughts for lighter ones right before bed. I posted every single blog post at 12:01 a.m. every day. Why was posting just before bed important? Because you know what happens when your mind is spinning? You can't sleep! And then how's the next day? Worse. And your energy and resilience levels the next night? Worse. And the night after that? Even worse.

The blog was a soaking wet shammy rubbed across the dusty blackboard of my mind right before I turned out the lights. I'd be brainstorming metaphors for what it feels like to take out your contact lenses. Taking your socks off after work! Taking off your ski boots! Taking your rented tux off after the sweaty wedding is over!

So what did I go to bed thinking about?

Slightly more positive thoughts.

The blog was a dot-dot-dot.

The blog was a way to shift the spotlight.

The blog helped me see things as a step as I tried to just keep moving.

3

Have you had enough one-night stands?

Blogging was a step for me.

A vital step. A necessary step. Because every single breakup hurts. It feels like the end. It feels like game over. My divorce felt that way to me. But it turns out that when you actually sit down with people in committed relationships and ask them to go backward, they always paint the road as a series of game overs that always, always, always continued.

A few years ago I stumbled upon a fascinating study published in *The Telegraph*.

A team of researchers was trying to figure out just how rocky the royal road to romance is, so they found people in deeply committed relationships with life partners and worked backward through their personal histories to see just how many relationships and sexual experiences had led them to where they were right then.

(Sidenote: What a bizarre research study! "So who did you date before Frank? Joe? How long were you with Joe? Did you cheat on Joe? Any one-night stands between Joe and Frank?" And yes this assumes you're dating the Hardy Boys.)

But it makes sense, right? Because everyone we kiss and everyone we date and everyone we sleep with shows us and grows us and teaches us and enlightens us and helps us continue down our lifelong journeys to understanding ourselves a little bit better and a little bit better and a little bit better until we ultimately become the richest, fullest, deepest versions of ourselves possible.

In that sense every single breakup has a purpose.

Every single breakup is a step.

Shall we get specific?

According to that study the average woman will kiss fifteen people, have seven sexual partners, four one-night stands, four disaster dates, three relationships that last less than a year, and two relationships that last more than a year, fall in love twice, be heartbroken twice, cheat once, and be cheated on once—all before she finds a lifelong partner.

Whew!

What about men?

Well, the average man will kiss sixteen people, have ten sexual partners, six one-night stands, four disaster dates, four relationships that last less than a year, and two relationships that last more than a year, fall in love twice, be heartbroken twice, cheat once, and be cheated on once—all before *he* finds a lifelong partner.

Does that sound like something you want to go through?

Me neither.

But in a way, isn't it also relieving to hear?

Because it may help shine a light on the invisible steps ahead of you on the staircase you're climbing on the way to the long-term, committed relationship you may desire.

I'm not saying it's easy! When I was living alone it took me more than a year before I started going out on first dates again. And when I finally did I was completely crushed when somebody I felt a little connection with or who I shared a first kiss with didn't text me back. I was fragile. I was heartbroken. The rejection destroyed me.

I became friends with a young gay guy who lived across the hall. He always had guys going in and out of his apartment. When I would tell him how shattered I was about someone not texting me back, he'd always have a huge smile pasted across his face and say the same thing: "NEXXXXT!" His words felt sharp, but maybe he was just better than I was at getting to the future faster.

4

"What's a blog?"

I wrote a blog post every night for a year.

I worked my office job during the day, then picked up takeout on my way home and went online till the wee hours of the morning before going to bed. I was grieving and I was reeling and I was processing, and since I was by myself, I didn't have anyone to help me flick the off switch.

First date after first date went nowhere. I started piling up the failures. I called the person I was out with my ex-wife's name. Several times. To several different people. I kept waiting for a slow and dreamy date to happen, full of long conversations, deep knowing smiles, and telling waitress after waitress, "Sorry, we haven't even looked at the menus yet."

But it never came.

I felt like I was living a Groundhog Day full of handshakes, hugs, and forty-dollar bills for wine and fries.

Another year went by, and I was doing the same things: blogging every night, getting introduced to people, meeting friends of friends, and having drinks with people I met online. One night my friend Rita, who lived down the hall, came over to ask if I wanted to check out an art exhibit across the street. She came over a lot to see if I wanted to grab a drink or snack. But this time she brought a friend.

"Hi, I'm Leslie," a stunning brunette with a giant smile and sunbeaming confidence said with an outstretched hand. "Oh, hey, hi, I'm, uh, Neil," I managed.

We walked across the street and roamed through a great photography exhibit before grabbing a glass of wine and a plate of fries at a French bistro.

"So Neil's a blogger," Rita said. "Maybe you've heard of his blog? He's been at it awhile. It's one of the biggest in the country now. They're turning it into a book called *The Book of Awesome*."

"What's a blog?" Leslie asked.

And I was hooked.

Later that night, when Rita emailed both of us a link to the photographer whose exhibit we'd seen, I reached back out to Leslie asking her out on a date. "How about Tuesday at 10 p.m.?" I emailed. "Or Wednesday night at 9 p.m.?"

"Sorry," she replied. "I go to bed at 8 p.m. I'm a kindergarten teacher."

"Well, how about Sunday breakfast then?" I asked.

"Sounds great," she replied.

And it was set.

5

Soak it up

A long, long, long time ago, tiny single-celled organisms appeared on Earth.

For example, an amoeba. Like this:

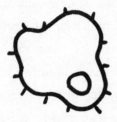

And then what happened? Well, 300 million years later those single-celled organisms evolved into multicelled organisms. Like this:

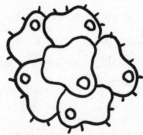

Then what happened? Well, 300 million years after that, those multicelled organisms evolved into plants and animals. Like us!

And you know what's interesting about this?

Single-celled organisms never went away. They didn't die off. They weren't rendered obsolete. Plants, animals, and our own bodies have hundreds of millions of single-celled organisms living on us and inside us. Our body is their home.

What about multicelled organisms?

Well, importantly, *they are built of single-celled organisms.* And, also importantly, they didn't die off but rather *became part of newer, greater wholes.* There are multicelled organisms in trees. In you. In me. In Oprah.

What's my point?

What we often think of as evolution "destroying and replacing" the past is actually "transcending and including."

The past gets soaked up to create the future.

The author Ken Wilber has put this idea forward in numerous books such as *A Brief History of Everything.* Cities didn't wipe out farms but rather incorporated farming in a more efficient and productive way. Movies didn't replace photography. Trip-hop didn't replace hip-hop. We didn't replace gorillas. Our evolved rational thinking didn't replace emotions but rather sponged up those emotions into our newly evolved rational brains.

Real growth, real evolution, doesn't come about through destruction. It comes from taking what came before and integrating it into a greater whole. What comes from burning libraries? Piles of ash. And what comes from reading the books and developing your own ideas? Pretty much all great thinking. What comes from razing towns? Piles of ash. And what comes from studying other countries' technology and copying it and learning from it? China. No, just kidding. I mean all future technologies.

There's no ride hailing without GPS.

There's no Siri without search.

There's no you of today without everything in your past. There's no you of tomorrow without everything you're going through now, either.

If my first wife hadn't fallen out of love with me, I wouldn't have moved to a bachelor apartment in The Hudson. I would never have met a girl down the hall named Rita. I would never have fallen in love with her friend Leslie. I would never have moved in with Leslie a year later and I would never have proposed to her a year after that.

I would never have gotten married to her.

And I would never have had a son with her named . . . Hudson.

I didn't know it at the time, but I had soaked up the past, and it created my future.

And that didn't just happen to me.

It happens to all of us.

It happens to you.

It happens to me.

It happens to us.

As you're falling, you can add a dot-dot-dot to keep going, then shift the spotlight so you aren't blaming yourself, and then finally, finally, finally try to

See it as a step.

ADD A DOT-DOT-DOT

SHIFT THE SPOTLIGHT

SEE IT AS A STEP

SECRET #4

Tell Yourself a Different Story

S o.

I fell, you fell, we fell, now we're here.

We talked about the three steps you can take when the rug gets yanked from under you, when you slip up and trip up and feel like you're falling, falling, falling, falling.

I hope those three steps helped. Maybe you didn't hit bottom. Maybe you're back up already. Maybe you're good!

But we all fall all the way down dark holes sometimes, too. Sometimes we really are at the bottom. That's where we come face-to-face with our innermost demons. Our private fears. Our guilty thoughts. Our darkest secrets.

That's when we feel like we're at the bottom of a well. We can see the pinprick of light way above us, but our hands keep slipping on rocks covered in wet moss as we try to climb up the sides.

Then what do we do?

Let's talk about the next secret.

Let's get a little more intimate.

Let's go back in time.

It was October 1979.

I was six weeks old and I never stopped crying.

When I say I never stopped crying, I mean I cried all day and I cried all night. My parents had no other kids yet, but they knew something was wrong. They kept taking me to the doctor, but the advice was always the same.

"Don't worry. Go home. That's just what babies do."

My mom was convinced there was an issue, so she took me to a different doctor who discovered I had a painful hernia and an undescended testicle. I was sent for immediate surgery.

"Will he be okay?" my mom asked the doctor before sitting in the waiting room and crying for hours while my screaming six-week-old body went under the knife.

I can't imagine how it would feel watching your baby taken in for surgery on his genitals in that emotionally vulnerable time a few weeks after giving birth to him. And I can't imagine what it would feel like for the baby either, since I have no conscious memories of it.

When I came out of the operating room, I apparently had no tears and no long-term issues, other than having only one testicle and a scar up my groin that would grow as I did. And because I was six weeks old, I never knew that had happened. My parents never mentioned it when I was a little kid, so I grew into a ten-year-old who thought all guys had only one ball.

Why?

Well, we have one nose, one mouth, one heart, one stomach, one belly button, one penis. There's a single-digit streak running straight down the middle of our bodies.

And as I think about it today, don't you think the human body is a bit strange with what it backs up with a second version and what it doesn't? Eyeballs? Sure, you're gonna need two of those. Get stabbed with a chopstick at a Chinese buffet brawl and you need seeing insurance. I get that. Nostrils? Two. Definitely two. Get a cold, and you need to breathe without your tongue hanging out like a golden retriever's.

Two lungs? Two nipples? Two kidneys?

Check, check, check!

But tongue, windpipe, stomach, heart?

Oh, one sounds totally fine.

So I thought my one ball was totally fine.

I lived without thinking about it in any way.

Remember: I grew up in the 80s.

There was no internet.

Ken dolls had no genitals. Cabbage Patch Kids had no genitals. He-Man had no genitals, though I bet he would have had huge balls if Mattel hadn't neutered him. (Think about it. The man rode a *black panther* like a carnival donkey.) Underwear models in Sears catalogues showed no discernable penis or ball outlines. Even detailed drawings of naked men, which I found one day in a copy of *The Joy of Sex* in a storage box in my basement, didn't have the testicular detail you might imagine.

Also, I wasn't looking.

I wasn't looking at naked men anywhere except in the mirror so everything made sense to me.

That all changed in ninth-grade gym class.

In ninth grade, I went to a large high school with a clear pecking order. Ninth graders were puny, had the worst lockers, and never got a table in the cafeteria. There wasn't a ton of pushing and shoving, but you knew your place and kept your head down.

Gym class was mandatory and I was assigned to the class taught by Mr. Christopoulos—a squat Greek caveman body-builder with short, curly hair, a unibrow, and a thick blanket of fur on his forearms. The man wore red Umbro shorts, a white T-shirt, and a whistle every single day, even in the dead of winter. He never smiled and was intimidating as hell. He might as well have ridden a black panther to class.

My gym class was made up of assorted 14-year-old nerds, hooligans, and punks, but nobody stepped out of line in his class. As if to cement his reputation, on our very first day, Mr. Christopoulos took our class to the weight room, where he invited us to show him what we could do. "Any of you bench-press? Go for it. See what you got." A few kids took him up on it, lifting the bar or adding a few light weights.

After everyone was done, Mr. Christopoulos lay on the bench himself and then kept ordering kids to "Add more weights!" until he was yelling, sweating, and lifting three plates on each side— over 300 pounds—while thick green-rivery veins bulged out of his arms and forehead. We stood in a circle around him with our jaws dropped and our eyes popped like we were watching Bigfoot give birth in a forest.

The message was clear.

This man would snap us like an Olive Garden breadstick if we so much as threw a paper airplane.

We fell into line.

Later in the fall, after a few weeks of weight training, track and field, and volleyball, it was time for health class.

Mr. Christopoulos took us to the music room and sat on the wooden conductor's stage at the front while the rest of us tilted cold metal music stands into desks and tried our best not to snicker when he started his straight-from-the-textbook sermon on menstruation, herpes, and AIDS.

Mr. Christopoulos was prone to lengthy asides where he'd wistfully tell stories about his days winning some European bodybuilding competition or pounding someone in a big wrestling tournament. Over time, our fear of him grew into a healthy respect and we started seeing him as the brawny big brother we all wished we had.

One day, Mr. Christopoulos started in on a story about how he was wrestling with a friend at a tournament when he had somehow managed to squash the other guy's testicle. Like, he actually popped the thing. The whole class erupted in deep groans and winces while Mr. Christopoulos just smiled silently, surveying the room, waiting for the noise to die down before delivering his big punchline.

"Yeah," he said, commanding every single eyeball for the big follow-up. "After that, we called him *half a man*."

Everyone burst out laughing.

The sound was deafening.

I was sitting beside a tall buzz-cut blond kid named Jordan who was my best friend in the class. He was slapping his music stand nearly crying he was laughing so hard.

"Half a man!" he screamed.

Kids had tears running down their cheeks at the one-two combination of the stomach-churning story followed by Mr. Christopoulos dropping his best joke of the semester.

I looked around the room and everyone was slapping their knees and tilting their heads backward while tears sprinklered off their faces.

And that's how I found out I had one ball while every other guy had two.

I mean, it suddenly all made sense.

I'd always felt confused when guys said, "It hit me in the balls." Why balls when there was only one? I thought it was just a weird figure of speech, the same way wrestling announcers say, "He got nailed in the breadbasket" or how people say, "I'm so hungry I could eat a horse" or whatever.

A stunning surge of feelings flash flooded my body. My innocent childlike acceptance of my body disappeared in a second. I suddenly had a physical problem. A big one. Right in *the very spot* where guys don't want problems! It wasn't like I had flat feet or a weird birthmark on my back shaped like Japan. I was missing a ball! I might grow up and have a high-pitched voice! I couldn't play contact sports! I might never have kids!

According to my teacher and all my friends I was *half a man.*

I switched from tightie-whities to baggy boxer shorts. I carried a new dread with me every time I went to gym class. I changed facing the corner of the locker room.

When the internet was just starting up, one of the first things I yahooed was "testicular implants." I discovered a world of guys who had had metal, marble, or silicone gel packs surgically implanted in their ball sacks for cosmetic reasons.

Can you imagine?

I mean, first of all, ball sacks aren't generally on display. So nobody sees them except a couple dudes in the locker room and, you know, the love of your life.

Yet this is what we do.

We take what's invisible to others and shine spotlights on it inside our own minds. That invisible feeling becomes the entire object of our internal focus, and it makes us stop thinking straight and seeing straight.

Half a man.

It played over and over like a bad song in my mind. It felt like a sharply intense liquid was soaking into my skin. I felt like a dry sponge dropped into a murky pond quickly filling up with cold cloudy dirty water . . . from all sides . . . all at once.

It took me a while to figure out the word for the emotion I was feeling. It was new, terrible, and dark, and it wasn't quite as simple as guilt or embarrassment or fear.

It was something bigger. Wider. Deeper.

It was shame.

1

The swamplands of the soul

There's a gremlin waiting for us in cold, murky ponds.

The Shame Gremlin.

Shame is at the root of so many stories we tell ourselves.

But what is shame?

The *Oxford English Dictionary* calls shame "a painful feeling of humiliation or distress caused by the consciousness of wrong or foolish behavior."

Mmmmm. No. Sorry, Oxford eggheads, but that's far too narrow. Time to go back to school and polish that up. Maybe get a degree from Cambridge or someplace. Because, first off, it's not just humiliation or distress, and it's also not always caused by wrong or foolish behavior, right? Shame can be caused by wetting the bed or not feeling skinny enough or walking away from a fight outside the bars. We can't say that is "wrong or foolish behavior."

Can we find something better?

What if we ditch the dictionary?

Carl Jung once called shame "the swamplands of the soul."

Swamplands of the soul.

There it is. Much better.

"Swamplands of the soul" doesn't easily fit into a dictionary, but it works because shame is really so many emotions stewed into a big pot: humiliation, distress, worry, embarrassment, guilt, loneliness, and probably others we can't even articulate. No wonder it's so hard to talk about! That little smiley-faced emoji with the red, blushing cheeks is nowhere near complex enough to capture the swamplands of the soul, the dread in our chests, the murky water soaking into us that is so, so difficult to swim through.

The researcher and author Brené Brown calls shame "the intensely painful feeling or experience of believing that we are flawed and therefore unworthy of love and belonging—something we've experienced, done, or failed to do makes us unworthy of connection."

We're getting even closer now.

Can you expand on that, Brené?

"When you walk up to that arena and you put your hand on the door, and you think, 'I'm going in and I'm going to try this,' shame is the gremlin who says, 'Uh, uh. You're not good enough. You never finished that MBA. Your wife left you. . . . I know those things that happened to you growing up. I know you don't think that you're pretty, smart, talented or powerful enough. I know your dad never paid attention, even when you made CFO.' Shame is that thing."

Swamplands of the soul, indeed.

2

Who's really to blame in the shame game?

Look. Shame plays a role in how all of us think of ourselves. We keep our shame hidden. We awkwardly try to navigate around it. We cover up scars. We comb hair over bald spots. Buy thick-heeled shoes to look a couple inches taller.

We all do this.

We all do this.

We wrestle and navigate and worry and stress about our perceived imperfections. I recently walked by a tabloid blaring a headline about an A-list celebrity who weighs herself *five times a day*. The editors plastered that headline on there because we can all relate to that fear, to being so debilitated by the anxiety and self-consciousness and self-loathing jackhammering in our heads, whispering that we're not good enough, perfect enough, whole enough.

So how do we lose the shame?

How do we grow out of it?

How do we move past it?

We can't walk around it.

We have to wade through the swamp.

But it's not easy.

In his book *Overcoming Destructive Anger*, the psychologist Bernard Golden wrote, "Some researchers suggest that shame comes about from repeatedly being told, not that we did something bad, but that we *are* something bad. Shame, like guilt and embarrassment, involves negatively judging ourselves when we believe we've failed to live up to either our own standards or the standards of other people."

My wife Leslie tries to be careful about this with our kids. She never says, "You're so messy!" Instead, she says, "You haven't put your books and clothes away yet." She tries not to say, "You're so forgetful." Instead she'll aim for something like, "You left your backpack at home today."

Shahram Heshmat, associate professor emeritus at the University of Illinois at Springfield, researched addiction for more than twenty years. He said that "in order to experience shame, you must have self-awareness that others are making judgment."

Sounds sensible. Sounds logical.

When the other kids were laughing so hard about the "half a man" comment that they were slapping music stands, I understood pretty quickly that they were making a judgment.

But here's a detail that might be just as important.

What if it's not just others making judgment?

What if it's us?

Sure, it's easy to picture a scolding parent or nasty teacher as the enemy. A friend of mine still vividly recalls the angry face his father made when he wet the bed as a kid. And I remember watching my seventh-grade teacher rip up a poor kid's spelling test after writing down O-D-J-E-K-T in big letters on the blackboard and asking the whole class what planet we all thought he was from since that's how he spelled "object."

We know those moments! They are the moments we can point at that create long-lasting shame.

But what if we participate in our own self-shame story, too?

How much do you blame others for your feelings of shame when the person actually internalizing, processing, writing, and repeating those is . . . you?

What story are you telling you about you?

What shame are you twisting into your brain all by yourself?

Research published in the *Proceedings of the National Academy of Sciences of the United States of America* states that "Shame is about how the 'self' views itself; that is, shame is not caused by concerns about others' evaluations of the individual." The researchers are suggesting that if you feel anxiety or worry about what other people think of you, that's actually a *consequence* of shame, not a cause of it.

What what what?

In other words, you wouldn't focus on how others see you unless you were already projecting some self-doubt and insecurities in the first place.

Let's go back to gym class.

Can we float above that scene and look at it again through this new lens?

While I was sitting in that classroom, I took the joke my gym teacher said and the laughs from my peers and crystalized all of it into a clear, concise message that *I* internalized on the spot: "My balls are messed up. I'm never going to find a girlfriend. I'm never going to have kids. I have to hide this from everybody forever. In summary: I'm no good."

I thought that! I'm not saying I got there totally on my own. What I'm saying is that I was an actor in my shame play.

And maybe I had a lead role.

3

What story are you telling yourself?

Seth Godin is the bestselling author of nineteen books, including *Purple Cow, Linchpin,* and *Tribes.* He writes one of the most popular blogs in the world and routinely speaks at places like TED.

I sat down to interview him for my podcast *3 Books,* and we discussed *The Book of est* by Luke Rhinehart, one of his three most formative books.

The Book of est is a fictional account of the four-day, sixty-hour Erhard Seminars Training that was a popular new-age movement throughout the 1970s. Seth clarified that he doesn't subscribe to the cultlike aspects of the course or some of the nonsense spewed in the book. Still, when he read it, something in it hit him like a hammer.

He summarized the book's thesis this way: "Your problem is not the outside world. Your problem is the story you're telling yourself about the outside world. And that story is a choice. If you're not happy with the story, tell yourself another story. Period.

That simple. And most people will hear what I just said and not change anything."

Is it that simple? Well, not always, but it can be. Because we often tell ourselves negative stories. We catastrophize, blame ourselves, wallow in our shame, tell ourselves we're not worthy, and worse. We write a story where we're the villain or the village idiot—or both. Why? Why do we dwell so much on the negative? Why are we so fast to judge ourselves so harshly?

If this sounds familiar to you, good. That's a step. Seth recognized his tendency to make up negative stories about himself, and once he did, he realized that his story was imbalanced, maybe even self-harming.

How can we prove that?

Well, I'm guessing that you probably won the birthday lottery. If you're reading this right now, you're alive, you can read, you have an education. Did your parents give you food? And shelter? Did you go to college? Are you healthy?

We can keep playing this game to remind ourselves how good we have it. This helps us recognize that most stories we are telling ourselves are skewed.

Do you hate your stretch marks? Can you try to see them differently? Can they be timeless tattoos commemorating how you brought your beautiful children into the world?

Are you ashamed of your dozens of one-night stands? What if they helped you understand your own sexual chemistry enough that you knew what you needed in a partner?

Do you curse yourself over the extra ten pounds on your gut?

Can you instead love the fact that you have a weekly pizza and wings night with your friends?

We have to remember that *we retain the choice*, we hold on to the choice, we get to make the choice to tell ourselves a different story.

We can rewrite our shame stories, we can be gentler on ourselves, we can take the kindness we preach ... and treat ourselves more kindly first.

Tell yourself a different story.

4

Tilt the lens

How does this work in practice?

How can we learn to see the shame stories we're telling ourselves and change them into something better?

We have to learn to tilt the lens. You need to tell yourself a different story. You tell yourself so many stories about yourself. You need to learn how to see the stories you're telling yourself from a new perspective. Through a new lens.

And how do we learn to do this? Same way we learn anything. Practice! Just plain practice. So let's practice together right now, and after that I'll share the three questions I ask to help my mind zoom out and reframe the shame stories in my head.

Here's a scenario we can use that I based on case studies in the book *Mindset* by Carol S. Dweck:

One day you go to your twelfth-grade chemistry class. You like the class, but when your test is handed back, you got a 65%. You're bummed. You tell your best friend, but she whisks by you in a rush somewhere. You feel brushed off.

Next, you head to your car to drive home and see you got a parking ticket.

How do you feel?

If you're anything like me, you're completely shattered.

What stories are you starting to tell yourself?

You're telling yourself, "I'm horrible at chemistry. I'll never get into college. My best friend hates me, and I don't know why. I'm so stupid that I parked where I shouldn't have. I am having an awful day!"

But when you look closer at the scenario, maybe you can start to see more context. Can you tilt the lens a bit? The chemistry test was just a test, not a midterm, not a final exam, not your final mark. How many classes have you taken where you bombed something along the way? I'm guessing lots. We all have.

What about your best friend? You feel brushed off because she was in a rush. You don't know why she's in a rush! Did she get bad news? Is she off somewhere important? Who's to say she wasn't rushing to class or had just gotten an important call? She didn't ditch you. She doesn't hate you. She didn't shove you or give you the stink eye. Have you ever been in a rush when a friend or family member wanted to talk? Of course you have. We all have!

And the parking ticket? It's just a ticket. Your car wasn't towed. You didn't get into a crash. Who gets tickets? We all do. It's a money making machine for the local town. They got troops driving around just looking for wheels a smidge over the line or a meter that just expired. Ticketers gonna ticket. It's not a black smudge on your record. You're not going to jail.

And that's the point.

Our brains are so quick to adopt the view that the indignities we suffer are part of some grand plan to upend our entire lives.

But they're not.

All we need to do is learn how to tell ourselves a different story.

"I guess I should study hard for the midterm next week."

"I hope my friend is okay. I'll check in with her tomorrow to see if she needs to talk."

"Oh, they ticket right at 3:00 p.m. outside the school. Next time I'll put a little extra in the meter in case I run late."

Is it easy to tilt the lens?

No, of course it's not. It's hard! Really hard. It takes practice to learn how to tell ourselves a different story.

So what helps?

5

Three big questions to help achieve this secret

I t's time for the three big questions.

These three questions help crowbar my brain out of the dark place it wants to nestle into and help me tell myself a different story. They work for me and I think they will work for you.

Here they are.

1. Will this matter on my deathbed?

I find this question helpful no matter what story I'm telling myself. And it's such an easy question to ask because the answer is almost always "No!"

So you had a half-dozen fender benders. Are you okay? Will it matter on your deathbed? No. It won't. Tell yourself you were just getting in some driving practice.

So you got fired. Sure, it's terrible now. But will it matter on your deathbed? No. Tell yourself, "I'm glad I had that experience, because now I'm better prepared to find a job I love."

So you mix up there, their, and they're all the time. So what? I do, too. Will it matter on your deathbed? No. Definitely not! Nobody will care about your grammar at your funeral. Least of all you! You won't really even be their.

Did you ever see the article in *The Guardian* about the top five regrets of the dying? Palliative care nurse Bronnie Ware witnessed thousands of deaths and shared the biggest regrets she heard. They were:

"I wish I'd had the courage to live a life true to myself, not the life others expected of me."

"I wish I hadn't worked so hard."

"I wish I'd had the courage to express my feelings."

"I wish I had stayed in touch with my friends."

"I wish that I had let myself be happier."

Do you notice anything about this list?

People on their deathbeds don't wish that they were prettier. Or that they had better spelling. Or that they had better abs.

They're looking back at their whole lives.

To soak up a lot of my shame about having one ball, I asked the question: Will it matter on my deathbed? The answer was a pretty clear "No." So I realized the shame story I was telling myself was really a choice. Proof? Well, here I am *shamelessly* talking about it.

Okay. On to question two.

2. Can I do something about this?

If you wet the bed as a kid and your father made you feel shame and you're still carrying it around, then sure, there are things you can do about it: therapy, counseling, journaling, talking to a friend, sitting down to talk to your parents about it.

Get it out of your system.

But if you feel shame about your bipolar disorder or your miscarriage or your inability to grow a beard, well, you may not be able to change that thing. I'm not saying that solves the problem! I'm saying that remembering you can't control them should help. Why? Because you're off the hook. There's nothing you can do. Now you can tell yourself a different story to help yourself move forward.

So you lost your wallet? Instead of telling yourself "I'm an idiot for losing it! Somebody savage stole it! I'll never trust a soul again!," try "Well, maybe somebody really needed help to be that desperate. I hope my wallet helps them buy a hot meal or a bed for the night." Is that true? Maybe. Maybe not. But it could be. It adds perspective. And it's a story that will help you move forward instead of swimming—and sinking—in the deep.

Let's try a more heart-wrenching example. This one hits close to home. A few years ago, my wife Leslie had a miscarriage. We were devastated, and the stories we were telling ourselves were causing us even more pain. What did we do wrong? Who was to blame? Was it this fight we had, that thing we ate, that place we went? Then we started telling ourselves a different story: "The fetus wasn't developing properly and a body is smart enough to know when it's best to end a pregnancy." Did that tilted lens, this new story, take away all the pain? Of course not. It still hurt. Of course it did. But by telling ourselves a different story we moved away from toxic self-blame—and it helped us slowly move forward and move on.

Maybe there really is wisdom in that old Serenity Prayer that asks God to grant us the serenity to accept the things we cannot change, the courage to change the things we can, and the wisdom to know the difference.

Because when you ask yourself, "Can I do something about this?," there are only two options, right?

If you can, well, hey, go do it!

If you can't, well, you can't. Why waste time worrying about things you can't change? I can't change having one ball, but I can do something about the story I tell myself. Leslie can't change that she had a miscarriage. But as a couple, we could choose to tell ourselves a different story that avoided endless wondering and finger-pointing.

And finally, question three.

3. Is this a story I'm telling myself?

Are you ready to get a bit meta?

Because this may be the biggest question of all!

This is about peeling and peeling and peeling away all the little stories we are attaching to the true facts in our lives. Because so often we're attaching stories to facts . . . *and we don't even know it.* Be vigilant. Search for absolute truth. Husk away all those mental attachments causing unnecessary suffering. Keep peeling and peeling and peeling until you find the solid and objective core, and then use that core to tell yourself a different story.

So I've got one ball. Some of you have one breast. Or one

lung. Or one leg. Some of you have anxiety or alcoholism or Alzheimer's. We all have something. The key to this question is separating what we have from what we attach to it. It's about finding the core fact and noticing that we're just telling ourselves stories on top of it. "I have one ball" is a lot different from "I'm disfigured with no chance of mating." The first is a fact. The latter is a story. "I'm an alcoholic" is a lot different from "My family will never trust me." "I failed my biology exam" is a lot different from "I failed my parents."

Those are the three questions:

Will this matter on my deathbed?

Can I do something about it?

Is this a story I'm telling myself?

It doesn't mean it's easy.

It just means that on our road to resilience, on our journey to awesome, on our path to getting stronger, we recognize there's an opportunity to be kinder to ourselves and we're able to use a few small tools to help us get there. Because the truth is that most of what we think is a story we're telling ourselves.

Only you can decide what story you tell yourself.

So tell yourself a better one.

ADD A DOT-DOT-DOT

◇

SHIFT THE SPOTLIGHT

◇

SEE IT AS A STEP

◇

TELL YOURSELF A DIFFERENT STORY

Lose More to Win More

When I was fifteen years old, I was invited by my math teacher Ms. Hill to join a merry band of overachievers on a nerdy pilgrimage to a week-long college enrichment camp.

A few weeks later I found myself piling into the back seat of Ms. Hill's rusty Toyota Corolla and driving three hours down the highway to Queen's University, tightly wedged between a couple of cute girls with pointy hip bones.

When we arrived for our week-long tour, we were treated to private rooms and all-you-can-eat buffets and told to sign up for a college mini-course. I watched the girls sign up for Philosophy and German while I went alone to Computer Science. But I was excited because the topic for the week was "How to make a website."

This was a big deal. I was actually going to spend a week making a website! The internet was brand new. And I got to spend the whole week learning basic HTML and JavaScript. The instructor taught us how to visit other websites and press "View Source" in Netscape Navigator to read their code.

It gave me an idea. *Maybe I can make a website that will be huge.*

I spent the last two days of the class giving birth to "Neil's Haven of HTML and JavaScript."

I spent an entire day getting the title to look the way I wanted it to. By researching HTML commands, I made the font big, *italicized*, bold, lime green, on a purple background, and, of course, flashing endlessly.

> **Neil's Haven of HTML and JavaScript!**
>
> **Neil's Haven of HTML and JavaScript!**
>
> **Neil's Haven of HTML and JavaScript!**

The site launched in May 1995. It gathered and shared all my JavaScript and HTML code to help others build their own sites. My whole goal was to answer important, pertinent, and crucial questions for other website builders such as:

How can *you* make your title flash in lime green?

How can *you* get an endlessly winking smiley face?

How can *you* add a perpetually bouncing ball?

Now, let's remember that this was 1995 and the internet was all chisels and pickaxes. We're talking *years* before YouTube, Google, Wikipedia, or Facebook even existed. Nobody had internet access except the occasional rich family with a Compaq Presario in the corner of the family room they'd use to dial up

Prodigy to show guests the slow-loading red Yahoo! logo. Everyone would gather around the thing like a campfire to watch ten giant red squares slowly load into a hundred smaller red squares slowly load into a thousand tiny red squares . . . slowly load into the word Yahoo!

By the end of the week I launched my site, and when my high school library got internet access on one computer a few weeks later, I was able to type in my website address—complete with numbers, backslashes, and tildes galore—and show my friends at school.

Jaws dropped.

Everybody was amazed.

Nobody had a website.

And look at that stat counter on the side of the page! It was already over 100 hits. Who were those people? Where did they live? What did they wear? How did they find the site and what had they gotten from it?

It didn't matter.

The high I got from those 100 hits was incredible.

Every chance I got, I went to the school library to check how many hits I had. Each time, I saw the number go up by a few hits. It took me a while to figure out that most of those 100 hits were from me during the week I had built the site, because there was probably no way for anyone else to find the site even if they wanted to.

But still, I begged my parents to get a computer over the summer so I could keep working on my site and we became a Compaq Presario and Prodigy family, too.

And then suddenly my website went down.

I guess some bearded dude in a Pac-Man T-shirt at the university computer science department cleared his cache or something because one day my website just disappeared. I felt frustrated, but I was hooked on the feeling of building and sharing something with the world.

Over the next fifteen years I started a lot of websites.

A lot of blogs.

A lot of ideas.

The goal was always the same: to see how many people I could get to come visit.

Fifteen years.

Fifteen years.

That's a long time. An eternity. **This is the giving and giving and giving and giving and getting nothing back the whole time stage.**

And how do we know when we're giving and giving and getting nothing back if we're really going the right way?

We can't see up the invisible staircase, right?

So how can we trust the path when it feels like loss after loss?

Well, we need to remember that losing isn't always bad.

Sometimes it's the exact step we need to be taking.

1

"Do it for free for ten years."

Sometimes I'm doing a Q&A after a speech and someone puts their hand up and asks a question along the lines of "So, congratulations on the success of *The Book of Awesome*. My question is: How do *I* get paid millions to write about farting in elevators?"

The question is along the lines of saying "So you won the lottery. How do *I* win the lottery?"

I always answer the same way, with a reply I stole from Todd Hanson, former head writer at *The Onion*. He was interviewed by Mike Sacks for the book *And Here's the Kicker: Conversations with 21 Top Humor Writers on Their Craft*. He said that whenever he's asked the smart-ass question "So how do *I* get a job writing jokes for money like you did?" he gives a very simple answer.

"Do it for free for ten years."

See, we're surrounded by tales of instant millions and lightning-fast growth and tiny startups sold to Google for billions of dollars two months after they launched. We keep clicking links promising the "seven 30-second hacks to get a six-pack in

21 days." We're desperate to pull back the curtain on Oz, but what we want to find—quick fixes, easy answers, shortcuts—isn't there.

We don't want to hear that some things *just take time.*

They just take time.

They take lots of failure, lots of loss, lots of experience.

So ask yourself:

Am I gaining experience?

Will these experiences help?

Can I stay on this path for a while?

Sometimes the answer will be no. Sometimes the answer will be yes. But the answers will help point out the fact that you are learning, you are doing, you may be failing, but you're moving . . .

So what do you need to do?

2

Lead the failure parade

In 1996 my friend Chad and I launched a site called "When I Was a Kid." We called it WIWAK for short. The page consisted of one-liners about things we believed when we were kids like:

> "I thought fish lived in my cousin's waterbed."

Or:

> "I thought those green power boxes at the end of my street were where they printed newspapers."

Or:

> "I thought the little thing hanging down the back of everyone's throat was to separate food and drink."

We posted our email address at the bottom of the site for people to submit their own WIWAKs, but nobody ever did, except for my sister, who confessed that she'd thought all dogs were boys and all cats were girls.

So not including me and Chad, the site had one visitor.

In 1997 I teamed up with my friends Rob and Tom to launch LabelZero.com. Our plan was to have artists upload music to our site for free and then, before users could download music, they would have to watch an ad or fill out a survey. Unfortunately, after we bought the domain name, the site stalled on my basement ping-pong table as we realized we had no idea how to approach companies, approach musicians, program the site, or do anything site related, in any way, at all.

Call it a case of ambitions exceeding abilities.

And let's pause on that idea for a moment.

Ambitions exceeding abilities.

Because the thing so often missing from the conversation around ambitions exceeding abilities is the fact that *it's a good thing.* That's what you want! Can you imagine if everything you did was easy?

Being ambitious means you have artistic vision. It means you can imagine what the end product should look like even if you don't know how to make it . . . yet. It means you have that hardest thing to develop, that thing that no amount of money can buy, and that thing more difficult than anything else to learn.

Taste.

It means you have taste.

And at the end of the day, taste isn't all that different from vision. Taste means you know what you want, you know where you're going, and now you're just somewhere along the muddy path to getting there.

When ambitions exceed abilities it's a clear sign you're on the right path. It means you want your podcast or your book club or the softball team you're coaching or the piece of software you're designing or the surprise party you're planning or the big report you're preparing . . . to be better.

And it means you know how much better it can be.

Wanting to be better is a real gift.

It means you're going to keep trying.

It means you're going to keep failing.

It means you're going to keep learning.

Sure beats doing a crappy job and being happy with it!

When I got to Queen's University I spent most of my time writing for the campus humor newspaper *Golden Words*. And when I wasn't writing for *Golden Words*, I was building websites.

I teamed up with a few friends in my business program to launch Ghettohouses.com.

That was my fourth website and it was the first one that gave me a tiny taste of success.

Everybody was complaining about the student ghetto surrounding the university. That was the name given to the thousand ramshackle houses full of raccoons and rats and covered with collapsing roofs and plastic tarps. The neighborhood was infamously run by a slumlord oligopoly, so my friends and I made a website where you could type in your address and write about your slummy rental. Properties could then be searched by landlord or by address, and over time, data from past and current tenants would add up to cases against the landlords.

We were going to help the people overthrow the system!

The site was popular enough that we got a couple hundred submissions. "Do not rent from Bill Lee!" a commenter would warn. "Our fridge at 105 Cherry Street closes with Velcro, our bathroom sink has never drained, and the upstairs bedrooms are on such a steep angle that my roommates are dizzy for an hour after they get up in the morning."

We sold the website to the university's student government for $1000 and split the money five ways. The student government promptly neutered the page to avoid lawsuits and changed the name to Student Houses, where every comment had to be approved first and nobody could say anything defamatory.

I was happy with my $200 but felt like a sellout and was frustrated the site died in the process.

Then came my blog on LiveJournal called *Taut Twisted Tightness* where I rhapsodized about the virtues of Granny Smith apples, chocolate Popsicles, and barbecue lighters. Guess what? Another failed site.

I'm on website five by this time. It's around ten years after I first got my dopamine hit from Neil's Haven of HTML and JavaScript *and I was still searching* for that next great high. *Ten years!* And those were just the sites I actually launched, not the ones I thought about and talked about with my friends all the time.

Did the pain end there?

Oh no.

For site six, I partnered with a former *Letterman* writer I'd befriended online to start up The Big Jewel. This time I paid a fancy graphic designer to create a brand and logo. We had a legitimate posting schedule—a new article every Wednesday! The whole thing was a knockoff of *The Onion*, McSweeney's Internet Tendency, or *The New Yorker*'s "Shouts & Murmers." We used the site to market our humor-writing services to magazines, newspapers, and other websites. Turns out appealing to a dying industry doesn't work. Over the next three or four years, while we wrote, edited, and posted submissions, we received a grand total of *zero* inquiries for our paid services and maybe a few thousand total hits.

Six failed websites over a dozen years. Six failures before I launched my next website.

My next website was *1000 Awesome Things*.

I had no idea at the time that this site would be the one to hit big. But it did. It won three Webby awards under the "Best Blog" category from the International Academy of Digital Arts and Sciences. It had over 50 million readers. It led to *The Book of Awesome* and a whole slew of sequels and spin-offs, all the way up to this conversation we're having right now

My point?

Lose more to win more.

3

What do wedding photographers, the T-1000, and Nolan Ryan have in common?

S ometimes it really is quantity over quality.

Have you ever asked an incredible wedding photographer how they capture such perfect moments? I have. And they all say the same thing. "I just take way more pictures. I'll take a thousand pictures over a three-hour wedding. That's a picture every ten seconds. Of course I'm going to have fifty good ones. I'm throwing nine hundred fifty pictures away to find them!"

I've already talked about Todd Hanson, a former editor of *The Onion*. What did he say? "Do it for free for ten years."

Seth Godin offers similar advice in an interview he did on *The Tim Ferriss Show*: "The number of failures I've had dramatically exceeds most people's, and I'm super proud of that. I'm more proud of the failures than the successes because it's about this mantra of 'Is this generous? Is this gonna connect? Is this gonna change people for the better? Is it worth trying?' If it meets those criteria and I can cajole myself into doing it, then I ought to."

Seth did another interview with Jonathan Fields on the

popular self-help podcast *Good Life Project*. He said, "I'm a big fan of poof." What's poof? The idea that you try and if it's not working—poof. You try something else.

This book is called *You Are Awesome*.

And what will I do if this book fails?

Well ... poof.

Onto the next thing.

Don't get me wrong. I want it to succeed! I'd like to talk about this book and the ideas it contains in interviews and meet people whose lives were helped or shifted or evolved in a meaningful way through this conversation. I want for that. I wish for that!

But I can't *determine* that.

All I get to do is *take more pictures*.

All I get to do is whatever I do right now and whatever I do next.

And that's the point.

I have to keep going with my next book, my next talk, my next project, my next whatever, whether this one is a hit or a poof. You need to keep going, too.

What do I know about getting to awesome?

One thing I know is we need to stop looking at successful people as if we're looking at products of success. At success after success. Because you know what we're really looking at? People who are just really good at moving through failures.

Moving through failures is the real success.

Building resilience is the real success.

The failures and the losses are part of the process for anyone who is willing to try. All successful people swim in ponds of failure. They swallow and choke on failure. They're covered in gobs of failure. They have sticky failure in their hair and under their fingernails.

So what's the goal?

Be like the T-1000.

Do you remember the liquid metal bad guy from *Terminator 2*? Take a bullet to your shoulder. Take a bullet to your thigh. Let it heal over quickly as you tighten your menacing smile and keep walking forward and forward. Watch out for vats of molten steel in the middle of the abandoned warehouse! Those really could kill you. But fortunately there aren't too many of those around.

When I was a little kid, my dad bought me *The Complete Major League Baseball Statistics*, a frayed paperback with a green cover. I treasured it and kept it in my room for years. I flipped through it so many times.

As I paged through the numbers, I started to notice something interesting.

Cy Young had the most wins of all time in baseball (511).

Cy Young had the most *losses*, too (316).

Nolan Ryan had the most strikeouts (5,714).

Nolan Ryan had the most *walks*, too (2,795).

Why would the guy with the most wins also have the most losses? Why would the guy with the most strikeouts also have the most walks?

It's simple.

They just played the most.

They just tried the most.

They just moved through loss the most.

It's not how many home runs you hit.

It's how many at-bats you take.

The wins pile up when you pile on the number of times you step up to the plate.

Lose more to win more.

4

The life-changing magic of hypertrophy

Hypertrophy.

What a strange word! For me it conjures up images of a two-foot-tall brass statue pegged on top of a Christmas tree–sized wooden base.

"Congratulations! You won the golf tournament! Here's your giant oversized cardboard check and a massive hypertrophy. You may need an Uber XL to get home."

But it turns out the word *hypertrophy* has nothing to do with winning a giant prize and has everything to do with how muscles grow in your body.

When you hit the gym and lift heavier and heavier weights you feel that burn. Grunt, sweat, and push your muscles to their max. To their limit!

What's happening on a microscopic level?

You are tearing your muscles. You are making tiny, tiny rips in the tissue.

Gives new meaning to the word *shredded*.

What's the takeaway?

Well, those little tears, those little rips, those little microtraumas, sound dangerous, but when you're resting the tissues repair which ultimately helps your muscles grow in size and strength.

Tiny rips. Tiny tears. Tiny failures.

Ultimately result in a stronger you.

Lose more to win more.

5

What every commencement speech gets wrong

D o what you love."

That's what the commencement speeches tell us, right?

"Do what you love."

Could any phrase be more cliché?

I bet if you had a computer analyze the most common sentences from every commencement speech in the past thirty years, there's a good chance that "Do what you love!" would be right near the top alongside "Oh, the places you'll go!" and "Carpe diem!"

But here's the line missing from commencement speeches: "Do you love it so much that you can take the pain and punishment, too?"

That line isn't mentioned in commencement speeches, and it's just as important.

Mark Manson, author of *The Subtle Art of Not Giving a F*ck*, says something about this on *The Marie Forleo Podcast*:

The reason I became a successful writer is because I enjoyed the work of writing. Since I was a kid, I was always the guy sitting on forums writing pages explaining why everybody else was wrong and being that annoying guy on Facebook who starts political arguments just cause. I love just spilling words out . . . things that other people hate about writing, I enjoy.

Mark grew up wanting to be a rock musician, but the pain of getting there—lugging equipment around, playing in dive bars, strumming the same chord progression for six hours—was never appealing to him. He didn't enjoy that pain. That failure. But he *did* enjoy the pain of writing and the little failures that inevitably come with becoming a better writer.

Do you love it so much you can take the pain and punishment, too?

The point is that you need to take the pain and punishment on the way toward the thing you want.

Do you want to rescue the princess from the castle? Then you need to be okay with rose bushes shredding your legs. Because if you're not, she's not getting saved. Do you want to find a new job? Then you need to be okay with the pain of handing out a hundred resumes and going to a dozen job interviews and being rejected by every single one of them except one. That hurts! But it's the pain and punishment on the way to a new gig. Want to find a partner? I hope you like going on a hundred bad dates and having your heart broken three times. Remember the study asking if you've had enough one-night stands? There is pain on the path.

So ask yourself the big question.

Do you love it so much you can take the pain and punishment, too?

6

Three simple ways to achieve this secret

Cy Young has the most losses.

Nolan Ryan has the most walks.

Todd Hanson says, "Do it for free for ten years."

Wedding photographers say, "I just take way more pictures."

And I just shared my story of starting endless blogs over years and years and years before I finally had one big pop. So say you're with me. You know failures result in more successes. We know that in our heads.

But how do we do that in practice?

Well, let's close with three key things that will help accelerate your failure rate and therefore quicken your ability to suss out whether you're on the right path, when you should turn the other way, and where you should double down.

Here they are.

1. Go to parties (where you don't know anyone)

Success blocks future success.

Say you get good at one thing and your brain, like my brain, wants to keep chasing that bunny. You struck oil? Pay dirt! You're on to something good. But the problem is that when you start making it and raking it, you're also *missing out on* all the other options, all the other efforts, all the other potential flops that might have led you to even greater success, however you define it.

Like, say you get into real estate in your twenties, you sell a few condos, you feel like you're really onto something. Great! But that also means you're gonna play the real estate game and maybe never fully realize that had you not quit ballet in your twenties, you might be on Broadway right now.

Success blocks future success.

The issue here is that when you're good at one thing, the universe conspires to keep you there. Stay in your lane. Stick to your specialty. It's nobody's fault. To move through this volatile and chaotic and ambiguous and complicated world we all need mental labels to filter and sort all the people in our lives. "You're my real estate agent friend!" your friends think. So when you chat with them at birthday parties, it's about the market and interest rates and when they should sell. All those endless conversations *serve to deepen your own knowledge* in this one area, *make you more successful* in this one area, and then crystallize your identity even further, making it harder and harder and harder to mentally break out and explore new ground and try new things.

What's the solution?

Go to parties.

Where you don't know anyone.

Accept the far-flung invite, hit a reading by an author you've never heard of, grab a ticket to a concert in a genre you never listen to, grab a cocktail at the hotel bar after your flight, attend the online meetup for an old passion you forgot you had and, of course, go to parties.

Will it be awkward? Uncomfortable? Sometimes. Sometimes, sure. You might not meet anyone. You could have three super-ficial chats and connect with precisely nobody. You may leave feeling like you just wasted your time. That's the risk. That's the downside. That's the potential for failure.

But what's the potential gain?

The potential gain is that you'll meet interesting people in interesting places.

The potential gain is that you'll drift into other lanes, you'll go down new thinking paths, and you'll slowly unfurl yourself from whatever mental sleeping bags you're rolled up in.

And maybe your experience will provoke and prompt new ideas, new efforts, new risks, and new ventures that you'll fail at and learn from.

Lose more to win more.

2. Have a failure budget

Set aside money for failure? Am I joking?

No. I'm not! Set aside money for failure. Maybe it sounds odd. But come up with a figure that you can use just to try ran-dom stuff. Assume it will fail! But try it anyway. Maybe $20 at an oyster bar, $200 for a boxing class, or $1000 to go to a distant music festival.

If it works for you to use an absolute number, great. That's perfect. But if you're not exactly a budgeter, I also have a mental model I use in my life that can be a simple way to think about this.

It involves deciding what figure game you're in.

Call it the **Number of Figures Game**.

Let me explain.

When I was starting all those websites, I was in the two-figure game. $10 to buy a URL? Well, that expense was approved. But nothing else was! I knew I was in the two-figure game because I had no money. I could afford two-figure risks, two-figure experiments, two-figure flops—but it ended there. I couldn't afford three-figure risks because I couldn't afford three-figure failures. And four figures? No way. So that meant no graphic designers for When I Was a Kid, no loading Ghettohouses.com onto a superfast server, no buying an hour of consulting from a retired music industry expert for LabelZero.com.

No.

I was in the two-figure game.

What was my failure budget? Anything that cost two figures.

When I started *1000 Awesome Things* I moved to the three-figure game. I was a grown-up now. I had a job. I figured if I wanted to try something, try anything, and it cost three figures or less—I would do it. I got stamps and stickers and postcards printed for my book launch campaign. I moved the site on to a superfast server. At the request of some radio stations, I got a (gasp!) landline to do interviews from home.

Some of those three-figure risks worked. Others were failures. **But remember: You win some, you learn some.** And do let me know if you'd like a pack of five thousand old stickers, will you?

These days my podcast *3 Books* is an example of my spending my failure budget. I really wanted to make a podcast that was ad free, sponsor free, commercial free, and just a piece of beautiful art. To me, anyway. So I spend around $5,000 a year making it. Flying to interview guests, production costs, recording equipment. It's a four-figure "failure budget expense" that I love spending every year. Why? Because it's vastly improved my learning rate, too.

Can you keep moving up? Sure. How high can you go? Well, if you're a hip-hop star or tech billionaire, maybe you're in the seven-figure game. The number depends on you. Your comfort level. Your risk tolerance. My goal isn't to tell you how many figures you should plan to spend on failures. It's to give you a mental model you can apply in your life to accelerate your lose rate and therefore accelerate your win rate.

Lose more to win more.

3. Count your losses

We always hear people say, "Count your blessings."

The idea is that when you're swimming in misery, it's a good thing to remember all the things you're grateful for to cheer yourself up. Do I believe in that? Absolutely! That's why I wrote *1000 Awesome Things*. I literally needed to write down a thousand awesome things to count my blessings and cheer myself up as I was processing the loss of my marriage and my house and the life

I had known. I needed to count those blessings to help my brain move forward and see it as a step.

But you know what we never count?

Our failures. Our losses. The times we hit the ground.

Writing this book was the first time I had to revisit all those old websites that bit the dust. When I started writing this chapter, I thought, "I need to tell people about the three failed websites I started *before* the big one." After I started writing, I remembered a fourth. While editing, I remembered a fifth. Then a sixth. They kept coming. There are probably others I've completely forgotten about because their half-life was like two weeks.

It felt good to revisit those losses.

They originally sat in a part of my brain that I wanted to delete. To not share! To keep quiet about. **But the truth is when we look at our flops we're really giving ourselves credit for all the learning and stamina and resilience baked into those moments when we made ourselves a little stronger.**

Counting up our losses and taking pride in our failures is really hard. Really, really hard. We are taught to hide failure, feel ashamed of it. And here we are talking about wearing them as badges of honor.

If you keep a journal, try writing down your successes *and* your flops. Be honest, and count your failures as they happen. Be kind to yourself by giving yourself credit for each one.

What do I write?

"I spent time and money launching a website and nobody visited. What a disaster! But I guess I did find a great web developer I can use next time. And I own the domain so I can try something new or sell it down the road. And today I yelled at my toddler. I feel terrible when I do that. I was tired and hungry. But that's no excuse. I have to remember I need snacks and time-outs just like he does."

Admitting failure is hard. But you can do it. Trumpet them! Be proud of them. Because you learned from them and they were the fumbles on the path that got you here. You wouldn't be here without there. And you can't get there without here.

This is really hard for people.

Because it means couples can't tiptoe around all their past failed relationships when they get into a new one. I'm not saying they should lay them out on the first date like a display case of painted ceramics. We don't want to confuse counting failures with plain poor judgment! What I'm saying is that once you've built trust in the relationship, *then* lay them out. Be honest and share what you learned from each one.

This is really hard for people.

Because it means leaders can't pretend their resumes are an airtight vacuum of perfection. "Here's the cherry-picked list of places I worked at with the cherry-picked results I delivered!" *Yeah, riiiiiighhht.* Nobody buys that. We know you're human. Do you know you're human? If you don't, then that's a bigger issue.

We don't trust people who haven't failed and we really don't trust people who *don't even know* they haven't failed or *like to pretend* they haven't failed.

We need to talk about failures. Flops. The more we have, the more we grow. So put them out there. The jobs you sucked at, failed at, got fired from. The relationships you failed at. The goals you didn't accomplish. We know they moved you forward. Share that. Share how. Not only will owning your failures humanize you, but being honest about your trip-ups and slip-ups means honoring how you got to where you are today.

Acknowledging that growth helps you recognize and appreciate it.

Do it for free for ten years.

Take more losses.

Take more pictures.

And talk about it.

Lose more to win more.

ADD A DOT-DOT-DOT

SHIFT THE SPOTLIGHT

SEE IT AS A STEP

TELL YOURSELF A DIFFERENT STORY

LOSE MORE TO WIN MORE

SECRET #6

Reveal to Heal

For the two years I was going to Harvard, I flew Toronto to Boston, Boston to Toronto, Toronto to Boston, Boston to Toronto, over and over and over again. The flight was just under two hours, and it was always on a plane with no middle seats. Just a long row of two seats on one side of the plane and a long row of two seats on the other.

So I always had one seatmate beside me.

Somehow that length of trip and style of plane often led me into an intense conversation with the person I was sitting beside. And I do mean intense. Like, the kind of conversation where the stranger beside me has tears in their eyes and whispers something like "It's time I got serious about my weight" or "I really need to see my son. He's not going to be young much longer."

Does this ever happen to you?

I think that happens to a lot of us.

On a shorter flight, it's not worth the investment. We're up, we're down. Who's got time for a deep chat? And on an ocean-crossing flight, forget it. We brought books to read, slides to build, emails to catch up on. We made eight hours worth of plans. It's like "I'd love to chat, but I've got crap to do."

But if the length of the flight is jussssssssssst right and the seating layout is jusssssssssssst right, your airplane row can turn into a little confession booth in the clouds.

Because when the conditions are right, we feel free to be ourselves. We aren't trying, we aren't putting on a face, we aren't aiming to grow *this* relationship into *anything*. We both know the whole thing ends with a two-second "Seeya!" in a couple hours. I don't know you, you don't know me, we will never meet each other's families, we will never meet each other's friends.

What a load off!

And yet we have each other all the same.

Lower stakes, less judgment, no baggage.

Makes for great chats in the sky.

Sharing with strangers.

One night on my Boston to Toronto flight, I made a strong connection with a bald, bearded consultant in his mid-forties. As he munched peanuts, we slowly inched our way into a discussion on love, relationships, and life.

Near the end of the flight, I said to him, "So . . . can I ask . . . what were your first impressions of me?" I just felt like those are so hard to get, and I had a sense that because we were being so honest, he'd tell me the truth. He dished them out straightaway.

"Well, you looked like a stuck-up kid," he said. "You had your earplugs in, your laptop ready, so I was thinking, *Oh great, it's someone who's going to quiz the flight attendant about the menu and then ask to see a list of ingredients in the hummus."*

We laughed and had a fun bonding moment, but I avoided asking for his name or for a business card so as not to shatter our fragile, anonymous intimacy.

Soon the flight was landing. Lights dimming, *fasten seat belt* ringing. Window shades pushed up revealing sparkling high-rises against a darkening blueberry sky. It was a modern sitting-around-the-campfire moment, just missing the crackling logs and chilly breeze off the lake.

I'm not sure what compelled me, but I turned to him and said, "Listen, man, we're never going to see each other again, but I felt a connection with you. So if you want to tell me anything, just to *tell* me, knowing that you're never going to see me again, for the sake of you, I just want to let you know, as your temporary friend, I'll be listening and happy to receive it. I know that's really weird, but I'm only putting it out there because I felt a connection."

And he said, "Whoa ... uhhh ... wow ... well ... Jesus ... well, you know I'm married, right? And, uh, well, I guess ... I guess I just don't know ... if it's right.

"I guess I just don't know ... if I should be."

I was trying super hard not to show any emotion and just receive whatever it was he was saying even though in my head I was thinking, "Oh noooooo," so I just said, "Yeah ... yeah ... I understand, I mean, yeah, tell me ..."

And he said, "This is gonna sound so bad, man, but I gotta tell someone. I know this sounds horrible, but I ... I think I'm smarter than her. I feel like that's the most terrible thing to say. It's just, I feel like we're not connecting. I feel like I can't be with someone who doesn't get my jokes, isn't interested in the same issues I'm interested in, doesn't want to see the same movies. So, like, it's a big deal! But I think the root of it is that we don't have an intellectual connection."

Pause.

Big pause.

"That's hard," I said.

And he nodded. "Yeah, sorry. I, I, uh . . . *thank you.*"

He crumbled back into his seat and I felt a titanic emotional release emanating from this guy. Like some thick piece of rusted metal, dripping in blood, had finally been yanked out of his stomach after being in there for years. Those words had been wedged deep, forever lingering, forever squishing around, and suddenly they were ejected . . . and now they could be tossed into a tin pan beside the operating table to be properly examined under bright lights.

His thoughts *moved forward a step* . . . and it seemed like he suddenly had a brand new field of thoughts to explore.

The plane skidded to a stop on the runway and we said goodbye before grabbing our bags and walking off the plane.

It was a deep airplane conversation and a beautiful moment, and I figured that was the end of that.

. . . but then . . .

. . . a year later . . .

. . . I saw him again.

As I said, I took that flight a lot. So I was getting off the plane in Boston, and there he was! The bald, bearded consultant waiting to walk on to the same plane!

We weren't going to be on the same flight this time, but I was about to walk right by him.

He looked right at me, and I looked at him. And when my face was a couple feet away from his face, I looked right into his eyes and could see he was stricken.

Like he was seeing a ghost.

He looked afraid.

And I immediately had the sense that he'd decided to stay with his wife. That he had buried his feelings deep or maybe by processing them had been able to see them in a new and more positive light. Maybe he realized he was wrong. Maybe he stayed with her for the kids. Or the money. Maybe he saw more complexity in the problem.

Whatever it was, I felt in that fearful stare that he was thinking something like "Oh no, here is that guy I told that horrible secret to . . . and though I wanted that secret released and disappeared and blown away, now that horrible secret is still alive and real and exists."

Part of the deal of the confession he had made was my promise that we'd never see each other again. And now, here I was, seeing him again. Violating that promise.

His scared eyes, tightening jaw, and stiff body language told me I should keep my mouth shut, walk past him quickly, and disappear as soon as possible.

So that's what I did.

And now I really have *never seen him again*.

So . . .

Why did I tell you this story?

What does this mean for you, for me, for us?

Well, I'll tell you what it means.

It means we all need contemporary confession.

It means that in our loud and chaotic world we need a place to let our thoughts clarify, congeal, and then fall right out of us. We get so bottled up. So tightly wound! We replay pains and problems so often, letting them swirl and spin inside us like tornados, that sometimes those pains and problems start feeling like *who we are* rather than simply *what we're working through*.

That slippery slope can cause us to stay at the bottom for a lot longer than we need to. We slip, spin, and get stuck there tormenting ourselves.

But there is a way out.

A little path to awesome.

1

What's the world's
fastest growing religion?

We have a lot of words and phrases for *physical releases*.

Orgasms. Giving blood. Sweating it out. Hacking up a lung.

But we don't have many for *mental releases*.

If anything, we mostly describe *how* they come out, but we don't have many words for *what* is coming out. Panic attacks, manic episodes, screaming fits. Those describe the *how*. Picture a Coke can shaken up on a scorching summer day and tossed high into the air before landing on a hot sidewalk. That's how so many of our mental releases finally come out. In a bubbling, frothy spew after our insides can no longer hold them.

Can I ask you a question?

Are you a religious person?

Now, I don't care if you are or aren't. I love you any way you come. The reason I ask is because if you're Buddhist or Christian or Mormon or Jewish or Muslim, you probably know how *confession* plays a role in your religion.

Yes, a different form of mental release.

And even if you don't know how confession works in a specific religion, you may know that it plays a role in religion in general.

Picture the Hollywood cliché of the mobster in dress pants and leather shoes getting down on his knees in the Catholic confession booth, staring through the metal lattice screen, and saying, "Bless me Father for I have sinned. I put Big Louie in a vice under the deli and then banged his wife."

Why is confession such a big part of religion?

Because, according to the Catholic Church, in addition to earning the grace of God, confession *provides healing for the soul.*

Healing for the soul.

Yes.

Many religions believe it's good to get it off your chest.

Confession is a form of mental release that is more of a thoughtful processing and less of a shaken up can of Coke.

Yet even though confession is an incredible mental release, many of us don't use it.

Why?

Well, according to *National Geographic*, the world's fastest growing religion is "no religion." Surveys show that the rise of "no religion" is happening faster than predicted. France, the Netherlands, and New Zealand will soon have majority secular populations, and the United Kingdom and Australia are about to lose their Christian majorities.

Why is this happening? *PLOS One* published a study called "Generational and Time Period Differences in American

Adolescents' Religious Orientation, 1966–2014." Yeah, it's a mouthful. But it reveals that today's millennials are the least religious generation in six decades. Is it because they're moving more and feel less connected to a church or temple or place of worship in their community? Is it because they're having smaller families, so they're not modeling and imparting values to children as often? Is it because with longer life spans they're a lot farther away from experiencing serious illness and dying family members, which religion has historically helped comfort? It may be some of those things. It may be others. Either way, it means that fewer and fewer of us have a religious confession booth to turn to.

And there's another problem: in addition to the decline of the church we have a decline of community in general. More Americans live alone now than ever before. A full 40% of us! And loneliness rates have doubled in the past thirty years. Typically the surgeon general warns us of massive epidemics like cigarettes and obesity. But in a *Harvard Business Review* cover story, former surgeon general Vivek Murthy said that the next big epidemic is loneliness. We aren't spilling with friends as much. And reports reveal we have fewer close friends these days than we did twenty-five years ago.

So then, in this age of rising secularism, in this age of rising loneliness, where can we turn for mental release?

2

A million postcards show us what we

In many cases, we are turning to one another virtually.

We share our stories in forums, reply to com
blogs, and even anonymously mail our confessions to
on postcards.

Really?

Yes, Frank Warren earned the nickname "Ameri
Trusted Stranger" after he started a viral art project ca
Secret in 2005. Every Sunday on PostSecret.com he p
curated series of anonymous confessions mailed to hin
cards. He has received over a million postcards to d;
have helped him create the largest ad-free blog in the v
nearly a billion views. PostSecret has also spawned a seri
selling books and a roving art installation that's been
everywhere from the Museum of Modern Art to the
ian to the National Taiwan Museum of Fine Arts.

All from contemporary confession.

All from collecting and sharing confessions and s
people around the world.

PostSecret is a striking and poignant reflection of the things we are bottling up inside. It helps show us that we need to reveal in order to heal.

I'm very thankful to Frank Warren, who graciously curated a little six-page spread of PostSecret postcards just for us right here. A mini–art installation in the middle of the book! Here it is:

That Saturday when you wondered
where I was, well,
I was getting your ring.
It's in my pocket right now.

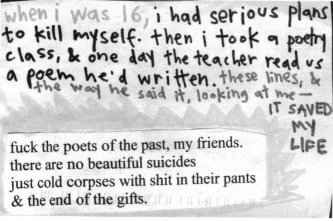

when i was 16, i had serious plans to kill myself. then i took a poetry class, & one day the teacher read us a poem he'd written. these lines, & the way he said it, looking at me —

IT SAVED MY LIFE

fuck the poets of the past, my friends.
there are no beautiful suicides
just cold corpses with shit in their pants
& the end of the gifts.

I WROTE MY WILL TODAY,

NOT BECAUSE IT WAS THE
SENSIBLE THING TO DO -

BUT BECAUSE I AM WORRIED
ABOUT WHAT WOULD HAPPEN TO
MY PURSE COLLECTION.

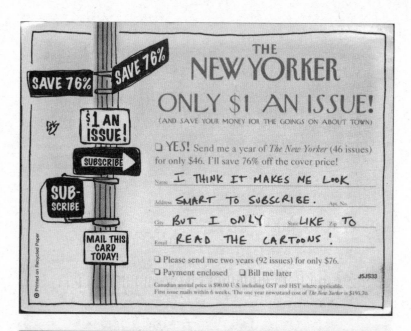

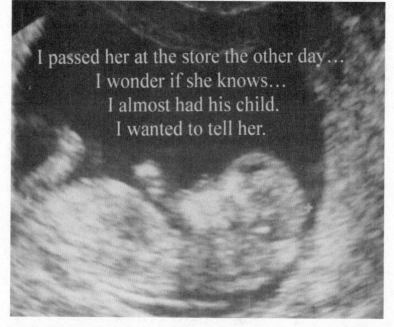

I used to work with a bunch of uptight religious people, so sometimes I didn't wear panties, and just had a big smile and chuckled to myself.

I am so grateful to the psychiatrist I saw when I was nineteen, who told me I would be fine again.

He saved my life.

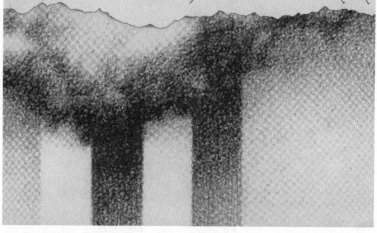

Everyone who knew me before 9/11 believes I'm dead.

Inside this envelope is the ripped up remains of a suicide note I didn't use. I feel like the happiest person on Earth! (now)

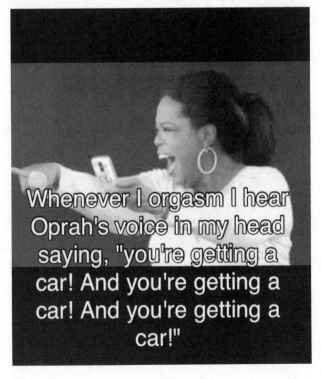

3

The two-minute morning practice

We must reveal to heal.

This is how we process things, tell ourselves we're okay, tell ourselves we're moving forward, and yes, tell ourselves we're awesome.

Reveal to heal refers to the mental release that comes when you *crystallize and eject* all the anxieties floating in the back of your brain.

When I first saw a therapist after my divorce, I basically bounced off the walls after each session in complete jubilation.

I had just spilled my thoughts—my anxious thoughts, my bizarre thoughts, my wild thoughts—whether they made sense or not. And my body felt the high of that crystallization and ejection. That reveal to heal. That mental orgasm! The process helped me sort, clarify, and confirm my feelings. And it ultimately helped me move forward.

It felt as powerful as any physical release I have experienced. As a result, *planned mental releases*—crazy expulsions of thoughts—have become a huge part of my day, and I've turned them into a regular habit.

Very few of us have any kind of regimen where we speak to a professional about our thoughts or do something conscious and proactive to help ourselves process them. Therapy is great! But it's far from accessible. There are very long waits for public therapists (if you even have them in your community), and private therapists are expensive. Understandably expensive! But expensive. Nevermind the social stigma. I get that social stigma is different depending where you are culturally or geographically or whatever. All I'm saying is that I remember the "What's wrong with you?" looks I often got when I told people I was in therapy. We brag about our incredible trainers or yoga teachers, but we rarely hear people bragging about the therapist who just got them to process all the guilt they've been carrying around since childhood.

So what's a more accessible option beyond professional therapy?

How can we crystallize and eject our anxious thoughts?

Contemporary confession.

But how can we practice contemporary confession?

I thought about this for a long time after that confessional experience with the bald, bearded consultant on the plane.

He felt so *relieved* after he told me what he was thinking about his marriage and then so *horrified* that that secret hadn't just disappeared back into the darkness. The insight is that we desperately want the relief that comes from confessing! But we also desperately want to confess in a safe way. PostSecret? That's anonymous. No return addresses. No names. A safe reveal to heal.

Some fascinating research published in *Science* magazine by the neuroscientists Stefanie Brassen and her colleagues backs up how healing it can be to reveal. Their study, titled "Don't Look Back in Anger!: Responsiveness to Missed Chances in Successful and Nonsuccessful Aging," shows that minimizing regrets as we age creates greater contentment and happiness. The research also shows that holding on to regrets causes us to take more aggressive and risky actions in the future. So the healthiest and happiest people are aware of regrets they harbor and then choose to let them go.

But how?

Want to know how to do this?

Here's the two-minute morning practice.

Every morning I grab an index card or a journal and write these three prompts:

I WILL LET GO OF...

I AM GRATEFUL FOR...

I WILL FOCUS ON...

I aim to complete the prompts every single day.

So in a recent entry, I wrote:

I WILL LET GO OF...
comparing myself to Tim Ferriss

I AM GRATEFUL FOR...
the smell of wet leaves out my door

I WILL FOCUS ON...
editing another chapter of my book

It takes only two minutes to do, and the difference in my life has been both *immediate* and *incredible*.

Completing three simple sentences helps me "win the morning," which helps me start to "win the day."

We're all awake for about 1000 minutes a day. That's it! So isn't it worth taking two of those minutes to help the other 998 be as good as possible? It's an incredible lever you can use to level yourself up.

Revealing a little mental anxiety on a piece of paper has been hugely healing for me. Because, crazy as it sounds, whenever we write out our little anxieties, they disappear.

I have five pounds of blubber on my stomach.

I'm worried about what school my kid will go to next year.

I think I said the wrong thing in an important email yesterday.

Want to know what happens when I flip back in my journal weeks later? "Oh," I think to myself. "What email was I worried about again?" I often can't even remember what the cause for concern was.

What about the big anxieties? Say your mom is sick. Gravely ill. These may be her final days. Will the two-minute morning practice still help? Yes. It will. Because you're saying it, you're processing it, you're admitting how you feel about it, so the heaviness can be examined and acknowledged.

Plus, the next prompt is "I am grateful for . . ." So you are forcing your brain to find little positives even amid a bigger negative situation. "I got to read my mom the book she read to me when I was a kid," "Nurse Jasmine brought me a coffee," "My kids all came home for the weekend for the first time this year."

It's a simple practice that allows for a quick therapeutic breather and a little moment of presence from our future-focused minds. The two-minute morning practice helps you feel better *and* get more done because you're performing a mental release. You're revealing to heal. Putting your brain in a better space. Showing up as your better self.

We know from a great study called "The Benefits of Frequent Positive Affect: Does Happiness Lead to Success?" by Sonja Lyubomirsky, Laura King, and Ed Diener that if you show up to your day with a positive mindset, you'll have 31% higher productivity, 37% higher sales, and three times as much creativity as your peer group. Those are big wins, all achieved by taking a few moments to let go of something, feel grateful, and bring some focus to your day.

"I will let go of . . . obsessing about the hairy birthmark on my arm."

"I will let go of . . . feeling embarrassed that I left the spin class completely out of breath five minutes in."

"I will let go of . . . worrying that I messed up my three-year-old by screaming at him to put on his shoes."

Revealed.

Healed.

And what about the gratitudes? Why do we have to make sure to write them down? Research by professors Robert Emmons and Michael McCullough shows that if you write down five gratitudes a week, you'll be measurably happier and even physically healthier over a ten-week period. And the more specific, the better. Writing down "family, food, and job" or something similarly vague over and over doesn't cause any spike in happiness. Our minds don't re*live* any specific experience that way. Try things such as:

"I am grateful for . . . Trooper learning how to shake a paw."

"I am grateful for . . . the cinnamon bun smell in the train station."

"I am grateful for . . . Rodriguez putting the toilet seat down."

You get the idea.

I picture writing down gratitudes after I've just ejected an anxiety being sort of like a Zamboni whisking through my neural networks, smoothing everything out, splashing freezing cold water over all my thoughts.

And now, finally, the focus.

What does "I will focus on . . ." help us do?

Well, once you've revealed and healed, cleaned off your mental ice rink, it's time to strip away the endless list of things you *could* do and focus on the things you *will* do.

Why? Because if you don't you will mentally revisit your *could-do* list all day long. And that will only cause decision fatigue. Decision-making energy uses a particularly complex part of the brain and we're wasting energy anytime we're unfocused. As Florida State professor of psychology Roy Baumeister and *New York Times* journalist John Tierney said in *Willpower: Rediscovering The Greatest Human Strength*, "Decision fatigue helps explain why ordinarily sensible people get angry at colleagues and families, splurge on clothes, buy junk food at the supermarket and can't resist the dealer's offer to rustproof their new car. No matter how rational and high-minded you try to be, you can't make decision after decision without paying a biological price. It's different from ordinary physical fatigue—you're not consciously aware of being tired—but you're low on mental energy."

Letting go of stress this way early in the morning helps me avoid mentally revisiting a worry throughout the day.

Writing down a few things I'm grateful for helps me be more positive every day.

And focusing my attention on a big goal for the day actually seals the deal.

Clean ice and clean thinking to get back on track.

Reveal to heal.

ADD A DOT-DOT-DOT

SHIFT THE SPOTLIGHT

SEE IT AS A STEP

TELL YOURSELF A DIFFERENT STORY

LOSE MORE TO WIN MORE

REVEAL TO HEAL

SECRET #7

Find Small Ponds

E ver suck at what you're doing?

Of course you do. We all do! We sign up for things we don't start. We start things we don't finish. We end up somewhere and look around with no idea how we got there.

Maybe you moved to a neighborhood where everybody is way richer than you and has a fancier car. You took a job at a company where everybody speaks in codes you don't understand. You got married and had a child with someone you're not sure you like. *We make mistakes.* Part of living is putting ourselves in new situations but sometimes these situations are wildly uncomfortable or end badly. Sometimes you just want to press the eject button and blast off to Mars.

That's how I felt for much of my time at Harvard. I respected the school, I was wowed by the professors, I loved my classmates, but I just didn't relate to the careers I saw grads heading toward. Why would I want to sit in a windowless boardroom helping a rich company get richer by telling them how to fire ten thousand people? Why would I want to help two companies merge just to satisfy some billionaire CEO's ego? Why would I want to slave away on a marketing team desperate to sell the world more air fresheners?

These jobs made no sense!

But then again ... they paid so much money. If the world is built on gears and cranks, a lot of these jobs were spinning them. I felt I wanted the lifestyle the school was leading me toward but at the same time it didn't make sense to me.

This is the context when I heard a story from Dean John McArthur that resonated deeply and which I think about everytime I'm trying to get stronger.

Let me share it now.

1

The life-changing story from the dean

When I got into Harvard Business School they asked to see my tax returns from the past three years to assess me for financial aid. So I gathered all the paperwork. And my income added up to less than $50,000 . . . total . . . for three years.

Why?

Well, I'd scored a doughnut three years earlier because I was still a college student. And I'd scored another doughnut when I was running my restaurant and couldn't afford to take a salary. And between those two goose eggs was my Procter & Gamble salary of $51,000 plus bonus. Or at least part of it, since I hadn't made it through a full year there.

I was embarrassed sending in the numbers to Harvard but delighted a couple months later when I got a letter in the mail saying "Congratulations! You are so poor we are going to pay for you to come here!"

Finding out I suddenly didn't need $70,000 of student loans felt like I'd just won the Powerball. But I'd received a lot of phone calls offering me free Caribbean cruises over the years so I read the letter again to make sure it was legit.

Turns out it was legit.

Turns out me and many other Canadian students were recipients of the John H. McArthur Canadian Fellowship.

John McArthur was the dean of Harvard Business School from 1980 to 1995 and, a Canadian himself, he established a fellowship to pay tuition for any Canadian who got into the school and wasn't sitting on wads of cash.

I felt an incredible swell of love for this random old man who I had never met, so when I got to Harvard I spent an entire night writing a five-page thank-you letter sharing my life story, my failures, everything that had led me to this point, and everything I wanted to do afterward.

Before I could second guess whether he wanted a super-long letter from a total stranger, I sealed it with a kiss and dropped it in a mailbox in Harvard Square.

A few weeks later I got a phone call from John McArthur's office inviting me to lunch with the sugar daddy himself!

I must have sounded nervous on the phone because the assistant had to calm me down. "Don't worry," she said. "He'd just like to meet you." Then she whispered, "We don't get many five-page thank-you letters."

So between classes a couple weeks later, I found John McArthur's office behind tall oak trees in a vine-covered building in a corner of campus.

I was escorted in. He swiveled around on his desk chair, smiled, got up, and shook my hand.

"Neil, have a seat," he said, and gestured toward the circular table in the middle of the room, where two boxed sandwiches were sitting.

"Hope you like tuna."

He patiently waited for me to choose from the many chairs to sit on and then picked the chair right beside me. He was wearing a casual button-up cardigan and thick glasses that wobbled on his nose. And he smiled so warmly, like an old friend—humble, gracious, down to earth.

I found this especially amazing as there seemed to be an incredibly famous painting on the wall behind him. Was that a Picasso?

He caught me looking at it. "Oh, that," he said. "Some foreign leader gave it to us as a present. We couldn't put it up in the dean's residence on account of the, uh . . ."

I stared at the picture as his voice trailed off and noticed it looked like a painting of a bull sporting a gigantic blue boner.

I laughed and we started chatting.

"So, how's school going so far?" he asked.

"Oh, you know, stressful. We started classes a few weeks ago, and I'm up past midnight every night reading cases and preparing for them. And the companies have already started visiting campus. Everybody wants to work at the same five places, so we're chugging beers with millionaire consultants and bankers with black bags under their eyes hoping we can become millionaire consultants and bankers with black bags under our eyes, too."

He raised his eyebrows and laughed.

There was a pause.

And then he told me a story that changed my life and, looking back, was worth more to me than all the tuition he was so generously covering for me.

"Neil, right now you're just an eager guy standing outside the beach," he began. "You're standing at the fence looking in. The beach is closed, but it's opening soon. You can see the sand, you can smell the ocean, you can see a half-dozen beautiful people sunbathing in bathing suits. But you know who's beside you at the fence? A thousand other eager folks just like you. They're all eager. They're all gripping that fence. They all want on that beach. And when the door to the fence opens, they're all running on to the hot sand and trying to seduce the same few sunbathers. Your odds of winning any of them over are so low."

I nodded. I had been through campus recruiting at Queen's. It was painful. Hundreds of hours researching companies, tailoring resumes, writing cover letters, filling out online applications, doing practice interviews, buying clothes for interviews, researching all the interviewers before I met them, writing and sending thank-you notes, and then the giant stress of waiting weeks or months for replies.

"So get off the beach," he said.

"Let the thousand other folks run in and fight each other. Let them bite and claw and scratch each other. And sure, let a few of them win over one of those few sunbathers. But it's much better to get off the beach. Because even if you happen to win, do you know what you would be doing the whole time on that beach? Looking over your shoulder. Seeing who else is going to stake their claim and send you packing. You probably won't win in any case. But if you do, you win a life full of stress."

I was in a state of permanent anxiety on campus. I was anxious about classes because I was anxious about grades and I was anxious about grades because I was anxious about jobs and I was anxious about jobs because I was anxious about money.

And here was this man offering relief.

"But if I don't land one of those jobs," I said, "I'll be broke. I got your fellowship because I didn't have any money. I was hoping to correct that problem."

He laughed. "You'll be fine. It's simple economics. **There are far more problems and opportunities in the world than there are talented and hard-working people to solve them.** The world needs talent and hard work to solve its problems so people with talent who are hard workers will have endless opportunities."

His words felt like calamine lotion rubbed on the bright red burn itching at the center of my soul. What he was saying was ... *different*.

"So," I asked him, cautiously furthering the metaphor, "if I leave the beach, where do I go?"

"What do you think you offer?" he asked. "You're young. You have little experience. But you're learning. You're passionate. You give people energy and ideas. And who needs that? Not the fancy companies flying here in private jets. It's the *broken companies*. The *bankrupt companies*. The ones *losing money*. The ones *struggling*. They need you. The last thing they're doing is flying teams to Harvard recruiting sessions. But if you knock on their doors and if you get inside, then they will listen to your ideas, give you big jobs with lots of learning, and they'll take you seriously. You'll participate in meetings instead of just taking notes. You'll learn faster, gain experience quicker, and make changes to help a place that actually needs help."

There was a long pause as I digested what I was actually hearing.

Think about this for a second.

Harvard Business School had an army of people dedicated to planning, executing, and guiding students through campus recruiting. It was a giant department. Career visioning workshops. Job posting boards. Information sessions. Beer nights and company dinners. First, second, third round interviews on campus.

And here I was sitting in front of the Dean who was telling me to set a match to it all. Ignore it completely and call up a pile of broken and bankrupt places.

I left that lunch and never applied for another job through the school again. Not a single info session, not a single job posting, not a single interview. I just went back to my apartment and made an Excel spreadsheet.

I filled it with a list of all the broken, beaten-down companies I could think of. Places that were doing something interesting but had fallen on hard times. A big oil spill. A plummeting stock price. A massive layoff. A failed launch. A big PR problem. Reputation in the toilet.

I came up with about a hundred company names. I then

wrote up a 30-second cold call script saying I was a student studying leadership and would love to ask a couple questions to a leader in Human Resources. I cold called all hundred companies. I got in the door with maybe half of them and then followed up with them to say thank you, share a couple articles, and ask to meet for coffee or lunch. About a dozen took me up on the offer. And after those dozen conversations, I wrote thank you letters and followed up asking for a summer job.

I got five offers.

And all five were from companies off the beach.

I took a job at Walmart and found I was the only person with a master's degree. . . in an office of over a thousand people.

Dean McArthur's advice paid off. I was suddenly a big fish in a small pond. All my peers from Harvard were long gone. They were crunching Excel spreadsheets in glass towers. I was sitting on ripped chairs beside piles of old cardboard boxes in a low-rise building in the burbs.

But I loved it. I had work to do. I had real problems to solve.

At Walmart I found I was one of a handful of people quoting fresh research and case studies since I'd just read and reviewed so much at school. There was a ton I didn't know. I had no retail experience! No store operations experience! No Walmart experience! But the things I did know were different from what my colleagues knew.

And different is better than better.

I spent the summer designing, planning, and running the first internal leadership conference at the company.

It was a hit.

Then, on my last day of the summer job, the head of HR handed me a full-time job offer with a primo starting salary pasted on top.

I was way off the beach.

And it felt great.

2

What's wrong with the $5 million condo?

What did I learn from Dean McArthur's beach story?

Find the small ponds so you can be the big fish.

When I was at Harvard Business School I was below average in everything. Grades, class participation, whatever you were measuring, I was in the bottom half. I was a little fish in a big pond of high achievers from around the world. I never felt great about what I was accomplishing there. I was always on the low end of the totem pole.

I think about this a lot when I see ads on the inside covers of fancy magazines advertising new Manhattan condos starting at $5 million. That's a little fish in a big pond right there! $5 million means you have *the worst condo in the entire building*. No view, no prestige, no nothing. Who would drop money on that kind of pain when $5 million could buy you a penthouse suite almost anywhere else?

When I started at Walmart, I was different.

And different really is better than better.

My degree wasn't immediately neutralized by being surrounded by tables of people with fancy degrees. At Walmart, I was *worth something*. So my confidence went up. My "I can do this!" feeling rose and rose and rose.

Don't start swimming in the biggest pond you can find. Start in the smallest. Don't chase the hot guy or hot girl at the beach. Find the nerd at the library. Find the broken company.

Find the place nobody wants to be.

And start there.

Dean McArthur's advice worked so well for me I started using it in other areas of my life, too. Sometimes it was conscious. Sometimes it wasn't.

But it always worked.

When I began doing paid keynote speeches, my speaking agency suggested a starting fee range that seemed super high to me.

"Summarize everything you've learned from your research and experiences in an hour, fly wherever people want you to be, deliver it all live in front of a thousand people, and make sure you're entertaining, educational, and empowering. It's a hard job! You should be paid well for it."

"I don't know," I said. "That seems too high. Who else is in that range?"

They listed a slew of people. *New York Times* bestselling authors, gold medal–winning Olympians, rock star professors. I'd heard of them all.

"Hmm," I said. "What about half that price?"

They listed a bunch of people I'd never heard of before.

"And what about half that?" I asked.

"There is no half that," they said. "That's the lowest range. It doesn't make sense for us to work for months and spend hours on conference calls and manage all logistics for commissions on speeches below a certain level."

"Okay," I said. "Start me at your lowest range, please."

The agency didn't love it but by giving speeches at a lower price I got booked for smaller conferences and events. I was in local boardrooms with fifty people instead of Vegas casinos with a thousand. My confidence went up. And it stayed up as I moved onto bigger stages.

I looked into the research underpinning the small pond line of thinking, and it turns out it's only thirty years old. Back in 1984 a study by Herb Marsh and John W. Parker appeared in *Journal of Personality and Social Psychology*. It asked a very simple and incisive question: "Is it better to be a relatively large fish in a small pond even if you don't learn to swim as well?"

The research in the study provided the clear answer.

Yes.

It is.

That study was the lead domino in a slew of studies around the globe that confirmed the same incredible result.

Regardless of age, socioeconomic background, nationality, or cultural upbringing, when you're in a smaller pond, your opinion of yourself—what's called "academic self-concept"—goes up. And importantly, *it stays up even after you leave the pond.* This is because two opposing forces present themselves: fitting into the group you're with and a contrasting belief of feeling "better than this group." Our brains like that second feeling, and it sticks with us as we realize "Hey, I can do this" or "Hey, I can maybe do *better* than this."

What's another way to think about it?

Ask yourself one key question.

Would you rather be a 5 in a group of 9s, a 9 in a group of 9s, or a 9 in a group of 5s?

The most impressive results of these studies say that being a 9 in a group of 5s increases your positive academic self-concept *even ten years after you leave the group.*

Put yourself in a situation where you think you're a big deal. Guess what? You'll think you're a big deal for a long, long time. And the studies saw these results across a wide range of countries in both individual and collectivist cultures around the globe.

So I say there's no shame putting yourself in situations where you feel really good about yourself. Should you downgrade yourself? No! Definitely no. But there's nothing wrong with entering the marathon in the slowest category. Playing in the house league instead of the rep league. Teeing off from the tee closest to the pin.

You know what you're doing?

Setting yourself up for success.

You'll move up because you believe in yourself.

Now, is there a danger here? Can you think you're such a big deal that you damage relationships or hurt others? Yes! That's the fire we're playing with. Do you ever wonder why so many celebrities get divorced after they first become famous? Maybe it's because their academic self-concept skyrocketed! They think they're a huge fish! And suddenly the small pond marriage they're in feels way too small. So they jump into a bigger pond and date a superstar.

Why do I mention this? Because it's about self-awareness.

We have to be aware of which pond we're swimming in and be kind as we swim. Finding small ponds isn't an excuse to act arrogantly and feel boastful. We're not trying to spike volleyballs into kindergarten foreheads here.

We're using a proven science-backed way to be kind to ourselves, swim in the shallows, and help ourselves slowly, slowly, slowly get all the way up to awesome.

Find small ponds.

ADD A DOT-DOT-DOT

◇

SHIFT THE SPOTLIGHT

SEE IT AS A STEP

◇

TELL A DIFFERENT STORY

◇

LOSE MORE TO WIN MORE

◇

REVEAL TO HEAL

◇

FIND SMALL PONDS

SECRET #8

Go Untouchable

What happens when you're getting back up?

Well, it feels great! You're hustling. You're grinding. You're cranking. You're burning. You're putting yourself in small ponds. You're seeing results. You're on the incline. You're being productive.

And that's a word to pause on.

Productive.

Isn't being productive *fantastic*?

The truth is we've never been more productive in the history of our species.

A 2015 McKinsey white paper on global growth says that in developed nations labor productivity grew 1.8% a year over the past half century, faster than in any previous period in history. The average employee generates 2.4 times as much in output as in 1964.

The pace of productivity growth is faster than at any other time in history.

And maybe that sounds all well and good.

But is it?

A *New Yorker* feature by Alexandra Schwartz calls our focus on productivity and hustle "improving ourselves to death." She writes, "It's no longer enough to imagine our way to a better state of body or mind. We must now chart our progress, count our steps, log our sleep rhythms, tweak our diets, record our negative thoughts—then analyze the data, recalibrate, and repeat."

Tim Wu, author of *The Attention Merchants*, wrote an article in the *New York Times* called "In Praise of Mediocrity" where he says, "If you're a jogger, it is no longer enough to cruise around the block; you're training for the next marathon. If you're a painter, you are no longer passing a pleasant afternoon, just you, your watercolors and your water lilies; you are trying to land a gallery show or at least garner a respectable social media following.... The promise of our civilization, the point of all our labor and technological progress, is to free us from the struggle for survival and to make room for higher pursuits. But demanding excellence in all that we do can undermine that; it can threaten and even destroy freedom."

Right now we probably soak in more information, communicate more often, and get more done in a day of work than our great-grandparents got done in a month.

But the trade-off is that we now feel less comfortable letting loose, getting creative, coloring outside the lines, taking wild risks, spilling paint all over the place, and tapping deeply into things that will ultimately matter more to us.

When the leader at your company cancels training or a

conference or an offsite, what reason do they always give? "We've got too much on our plates right now." You can picture the stern look and furrowed eyebrows and roomful of people nodding. "Oh yes. Plates full. Very busy. No more can do."

We feel like we can't afford to stick a twig in the spokes of our productivity wheel or the bike will go tumbling down the hill.

We are so tightly wound!

But we can stop it.

We have to stick the twig in our own spokes.

Yes, one way we need to get to awesome is by mastering the ability to turn off the noise from everything around us in order to sit in those tiny little ponds of tranquillity where our thoughts and ideas can scramble and ferment and marinate and grow . . .

We need to find space. Space where we can escape. Space where we can process. Space where we can reflect. Space where we can get off the deck, climb up to the captain's chair, and make sure our ship is really going the right way.

How do we do it?

Untouchable Days.

1

The two questions you must ask before you quit your job

How do you know when you need Untouchable Days?

I'll tell you what happened to me after I quit my job at Walmart after a decade there.

First, why did I quit?

Well, it's based on the three bucket idea I share in *The Happiness Equation*. Lemme share a quick version now.

A week has 168 hours in it. A 56-hour bucket for your busy job, a 56-hour bucket for sleep, and a 56-hour bucket for fun.

The work bucket and sleep bucket pay for, justify, and create the third bucket—the fun bucket. The anything-you-want bucket!

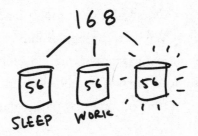

For most of my decade at Walmart my third bucket was writing my blog *1000 Awesome Things*, writing *The Book of Awesome* and its sequels, and giving speeches about those projects. Call it a hobby, call it a side hustle, call it whatever you want. All that early work on intentional living was actually part of my fun bucket.

But after I settled down with Leslie and we had kids, my third bucket started filling up with bath, book, and bedtime. Suddenly I couldn't be an evening and weekend writer anymore. Basically, I ran out of buckets and needed to decide if my 56-hour-a-week work bucket would go to Walmart or my writing and speaking.

What happened?

With the help of an old mentor I crafted a simple two-question model to help make the decision. I share these two questions because I think they can be helpful whenever you're deciding to make the leap. A leap. Any leap.

Before you jump, ask yourself:

1. **The Regret Question:** What will I regret not doing more when I look at it from the future?
2. **The Plan B Question:** What will I do if it fails?

For me, the answers came clearly.

On the Regret Question: Even though I was climbing the corporate ladder at Walmart, the opportunity to dig deep and write and talk about my passion for intentional living was a wild and rare opportunity. I knew if I stubbed out that flame to become a corporate C-suiter, some nagging regret might torture me forever.

On the Plan B Question: What would I do if I chose to write and failed? If book after book bombed? If my publisher ditched me? If everyone unfollowed me? If I tipped into the dustbin of loud talkers from years gone by who eventually faded to mute? It could happen. Still can! But I knew I could polish off the resume and go door knocking again. It took time to process and confirm that thought, but ultimately I had faith I could find another job.

So I made the decision.

I quit Walmart and moved my 56-hour fun bucket over to the 56-hour work bucket. Still 56 hours for sleep! And what did the fun bucket become? Bath, book, and bedtime. Being around! Hanging with my family. Trying (trying) to be a great husband and dad.

The two questions felt right.

And the idea looked good on paper.

But there was just one problem.

2

The barrage is getting louder

In my first year after quitting my day job, I actually found my writing productivity *slipping*.

Why?

Because while I had been picturing my writing life as this airy landscape of endless alone time, it actually immediately got filled up with meetings. Meetings? Turns out they never really go away. Research calls and phone interviews and lunches with agents and coffees with web developers and conference calls about publishing schedules and radio interviews and media prep calls.

So what happened?

Well, my writing would stop and stutter all day. The engine never quite revved. The problem, of course, the big problem, was that I was now measured solely on my creative output.

Yet I had no time for creative output.

It wasn't just disheartening. It was embarrassing!

"So how's the new book coming along?"

"Oh, now that I quit my job? Terribly!"

I thought I was creating space by quitting my job. But I was actually just creating more room for endless meetings and distractions to quickly fill the void.

It's not just me, either.

It's a problem we all face today.

And it's getting worse.

As our world gets busier and our phones get beepier, the scarcest resource of all is quickly becoming attention.

And everybody wants a piece!

We are living in a world where a hundred tiny hooks are fishing for our brains all day. Get on a plane, and an unstoppable, unpausable, unmutable luxury car ad is screaming from the back of the seat in front of you. Before you get off the flight, the attendant rambles through a long robotic script asking you to *sign up now* for the airline's credit card. Step into the elevator, and the little TV in the corner is selling you insurance while offering up the weather and spastic news headlines as bait for your eyeballs. Walk into a hotel room and the TV is beckoning you down to the bar before you set your laptop on a desk full of tent cards for hot stone massages and coconut shrimp appetizers at the restaurant in the lobby. Peek at the text popping up on your phone and it's your telecom company cheerfully informing you that you're going over your data but if you press "1" now you can add more for $10. Open your email inbox and four spammy newsletters have arrived since you last checked. Stare out the window and see a bus driving by wrapped in a giant ad for the new superhero mega-movie right below a forest of billboards advertising ninety-nine-cent chicken sandwiches, downtown strip clubs, and paternity tests.

How are we supposed to focus?

3

How to disappear completely

I found my writing time completely gone.

I thought back to my blogging days and realized I used to be one of those "wake up at 4:00 a.m." or "keep chugging till 4:00 a.m." guys who just grinds away while everybody else sleeps. It's how I wrote a thousand blog posts in a thousand days. But now I understand you can only drive in the express lane for so long before the wheels come off. And I find myself resisting advice from people who don't seem to be making time for those crucial buckets of sleep and family.

I realized that what I needed was a *practical* way to get more work done without taking more time.

And I needed it fast.

Well, I finally found a solution that I feel has saved my career, my time, and my sanity.

I bet you need this solution, too.

I call it "Untouchable Days."

These are days when I am literally 100% unreachable in any way . . . by anyone.

What are the results?

Well, Untouchable Days have become my secret weapon. To share a rough comparison, on a day when I write between meetings, I'll write about 500 words a day. On an Untouchable Day, it's not unusual for me to write 5000 words. Ten times more! And I'm on a high all week because I hit my writing goals.

Why am I ten times more productive on Untouchable Days?

A fascinating 2009 paper by University of Minnesota business professor Sophie Leroy found that getting into a flow state while doing *a single task* enables us to be more productive than when we try to focus on *multiple tasks*.

Leroy coined the term *attention residue* to explain why we're less productive when we have lots of meetings and tons of different tasks to accomplish in a given day. Basically, a residue of our attention gets stuck thinking about the last task we were doing.

When I start chatting with people about Untouchable Days, they start laughing.

Why?

Because we are all getting hundreds of emails and texts and dings and pings a day and juggling so many competing assignments and projects and priorities that it seems wholly laughable to even imagine walking away from it all.

But it is possible.

And vital.

Let me share what Untouchable Days look like up close.

I think of them as having two components.

1. There is the deep creative work.

When you're in the zone, your brain is buzzing, you're in a state of flow, and the big project you're working on is getting accomplished step by step by step.

2. There are the little nitros.

Little blasts of fuel you can use to prime your own pump or open up your creative centers if you hit a wall. Those unproductive moments of frustration happen to all of us, and it's less important to avoid them than to have a mental toolkit you can whip out when they occur. What are my tools? Heading to the gym for a workout. Grabbing a pack of almonds. Going on a nature walk. Doing a ten-minute meditation. Switching to a new work space.

How do I carve out Untouchable Days? I look at my calendar *sixteen weeks* ahead of today, and for each week, I block out an entire day as UNTOUCHABLE. I put it in all caps, too: UNTOUCHABLE. I don't write in all caps for anything else, but I allow UNTOUCHABLE days to scream out to me.

Why sixteen weeks ahead? The number of weeks isn't as important as the thinking behind it. For me, that's after my speaking schedule is locked in—but, importantly, before anything else is. That's a magic moment in my schedule. It's the perfect time to plant the Untouchable Day flag before anything else can claim that spot.

On the actual Untouchable Day itself, I picture myself sitting in a car surrounded by two inches of thick, bulletproof glass on all sides. Nothing gets in. Nothing gets out. Meetings bounce off the windshield. Texts, alerts, and phone calls, too. My cell phone is in airplane mode all day. My laptop has Wi-Fi disabled. Not a single thing can bother me. And not a single thing does. So I'm able to dive easily, freely, and deeply into my work.

So what happens if the bulletproof car of an Untouchable Day gets bumped? Say I get an incredible invitation or somebody much more important than me really has only *that one day* to get together?

Red alert: the Untouchable Day is under threat.

What do I do?

I have a simple rule. Untouchable Days may never be deleted, but they can move between the bumpers of the weekends. They can't jump weeks, though. They are more important than anything else I am doing, so if they need to move from a Wednesday to a Thursday or a Friday, that's fine—even if I have to move four meetings to make room. The beauty of this approach is that when you plant the Untouchable Day flag on your calendar, it really does feel permanent. You start feeling the creative high you'll get from deep output as soon as you book them in.

And my Untouchable Days have more structure around them to make sure they actually happen!

4

The 3 excuses you'll get when attempting this secret

Like I said, when I tell people to go untouchable, they have all kinds of objections. But this! But that! Well, let's talk about them.

The first but. The big but!

But what about emergencies?

Well, the short answer is that there never really are any. The long answer is that when Leslie asked me about emergencies, she didn't love my rant about how back in the day nobody had cell phones and we were all unreachable at times. Our culture is so oriented to worst-case-scenario worrying that some people can no longer imagine not tracking their children's cell phone locations or wondering how to reach a spouse if they fall off their bike. I say: Please. People need to chill. This fear-based, worry-oriented, what-if-disaster-strikes culture needs a cold bucket of water splashed on it quick. Our adrenal glands are fritzed out. We're all on high alert. But I get that we're in relationships, so when I started doing this, as a compromise to my wife, I told her that when I had an Untouchable Day, I'd open the door of my bulletproof car for an hour at lunchtime.

What happened when I did?

I came face-to-face with the whizzing bullets of seventeen text messages, dozens of urgent-sounding emails, endless robo-generated alerts and feeds—and precisely zero emergencies from my wife. So after a few months we stopped doing that and I just started telling her where I'd be. That gave her peace of mind that, if something happened, as a last resort she could call the place where I was working or simply drive over and find me. I've pulled off Untouchable Days for a couple of years now. Nothing horrible has ever happened, and Leslie and I have both grown more comfortable with zero contact throughout the day.

Next but!

But what about urgent meetings?

I have someone I need to talk to every day. I have a job where it's very, very important that I'm always, always available. Okay! I hear you. You're a doctor in the ER. You're the assistant to the boss. I hear you. So the solution here is to start small. Try an Untouchable Lunch. One where you don't eat with everybody in the cafeteria but you go for a long stroll. Or try an Untouchable Morning. Regardless of your role or position, you will gain much needed perspective, finally tackle a long-procrastinated project, or gain insight into a new way of working that convinces everybody else that your untouchable work times are valuable, too.

What's a side benefit here? Well, in jobs where the team or group of people around you helps you get an Untouchable Lunch or Untouchable Morning, guess what? You get to pay back the favor and help cover them when they take one. Untouchable Days actually strengthen team bonds.

And the final but?

I really want people on my team to take Untouchable Days, but *they* have trouble disconnecting.

This is interesting and actually pretty common. This but is referring to people who answer emails on vacation. It sounds like servant leadership but it's actually egotistical because they think they're saying "I am a warrior for the team!" but what they're actually saying is "I am so important that nobody can work without me!" and also "I am unable to come back with new thoughts and fresh ideas because I refuse to get out of the trenches!"

I did a study with a company called SimpliFlying where we tested the effects of *mandatory* vacations. We published the results in *Harvard Business Review* and found that creating penalties for contacting the office worked really well. Yes, we actually docked people's paid vacation days if they contacted the office on their days off. So want your direct report to go untouchable? Tell them to leave their computer and cell phone at the office and tell them they'll get dinged if they keep reaching out.

Remember: Untouchable Days are possible.

And vital.

Before I embraced Untouchable Days, I treaded water. I wrote articles, I gave speeches, I got things done. But something was missing. When I implemented Untouchable Days, magic happened. I danced sideways and backward. I did things I never thought I'd do! I wrote *You Are Awesome*, I wrote a new keynote speech, I drafted proposals for my next few books, and I started my *3 Books* podcast.

We have to stick the twig in our own spokes.

We have to learn to turn down the noise and find little ponds of tranquillity where our thoughts can scramble and ferment and congeal in order to help us reflect and make sure we're going the right way.

This is crucial to our own growth.

This is crucial to getting to awesome.

You know how I stick the twig in my own spokes and you know why I think there are real benefits to doing so. So you may be wondering, with a couple years of Untouchable Days under my belt, do I *still* go through all the work of carefully scheduling out and protecting and preserving one Untouchable Day every single week?

To be honest, the answer is no.

Now I schedule two.

ADD A DOT-DOT-DOT

SHIFT THE SPOTLIGHT

SEE IT AS A STEP

TELL YOURSELF A DIFFERENT STORY

LOSE MORE TO WIN MORE

REVEAL TO HEAL

FIND SMALL PONDS

GO UNTOUCHABLE

SECRET #9

Never, Never Stop

H ere we are.

The final secret.

The last spin on the merry-go-round.

So far we have talked about so many ways to build resilience, from adding a dot-dot-dot to shifting the spotlight to losing more to win more to finding small ponds to going untouchable. This whole journey has been a ride. And we're all on a ride together. My mom got on the ride before me and we started with her story.

And my dad got on the ride before me, too.

So let's finish by going full circle.

Let's finish with a final secret that underpins every other message in this book.

My dad was born Surinder Kumar Pasricha in a village called Tarn Taran in India in 1944.

If you ask him his birthday he'll tell you he doesn't know

it. They didn't keep records back then. One day you weren't there. The next day you were.

Nobody thought it was worth writing down.

I guess there were a lot of kids and not many notebooks.

It's funny that I didn't learn the basics of my dad's life—name, place of birth, date of birth—until I was grown up.

I always thought my dad was born in New Delhi until one day in my late twenties when I was mindlessly flipping channels at my sister's place and a scene from the movie *Gandhi* popped up showing the famous golden temple of Amritsar, India.

"That's where I was born," my dad said. "Actually, a small village near there called Tarn Taran."

I was confused. "What? I thought you were from New Delhi?"

"No, no," he said. "I *grew up* in New Delhi, I *went to school* in New Delhi."

"But you always tell people you're from New Delhi when they ask."

"Neil," he said with a sigh, "that's just easier. Everybody has heard of New Delhi."

That's just easier.

Those were famous words from my dad.

But it wasn't just his hometown he made easier. It was his name, too.

When he first started teaching physics and math at Dunbarton High School in Pickering, Ontario, none of the teachers could pronounce his name. Nobody could say "Surinder" properly.

They called him Surrender instead.

Surrender.

Soon after he arrived in Canada he said to himself, "I didn't come all this way to *surrender*. I came here to grow, to learn, to get better."

The next time a teacher in the staff room asked what his name was, he offered his middle name instead. "Kumar, but you can call me Ken."

Ken. *Can*. That sounded better to him.

No Surinder. I Ken.

No surrender. I can.

And now he's been Ken for almost fifty years.

My dad gave my sister and me our names, Nina and Neil, because they were easy to spell, easy to pronounce, easy to say, to write, to live with. Sure, he loved the names his siblings gave their kids, who also grew up near Toronto, beautiful Indian names like Ajai, Rajeev, Rajash, Nishant, Vinita, Manju.

But he wanted to fit in.

He wanted *us* to fit in.

So those names weren't for him.

Why?

Because *that's just easier.*

Researcher Brené Brown has called us the most "sorted" generation in history. Sorted. As in, we all sit in different value systems and ideals and affiliations, and if you're not *with us*, you're *against us*. So much sorting! So much animosity.

Adopting a view like my dad's—doing things that might just be *easier* for other people—is a generous way to live. It doesn't mean shredding your values or dishonoring your traditions or snapping open your moral compass and flicking the little arrow. No! It doesn't mean giving up parts of yourself that you value. It just means when you can make things easier for other people at no cost to yourself . . . you do it.

1

There is magic in doing things simply

My dad grew up in a small clapboard house on a sandy side street and shared a tiny bedroom with his three brothers and one sister. He was only three when his mom died of unknown causes and the family suddenly had trouble making ends meet.

With his father running a Singer sewing machine shop in nearby Amritsar, my dad's aging grandmother came to watch him and his siblings, who were taught to scrimp, save, and raise one another for twenty years. My dad had one sister named Swedesh. And what were the four brothers' names? Vijay, Ravinder, Jatinder, and Surinder.

I'm serious!

You can't make that up.

School was important, and math was my dad's specialty. Times tables and algebra were done on a slate, *The Pickwick Papers* was assigned reading, and gym class consisted of running around a schoolyard full of pebbles and crab grass.

In the evenings he worked long hours ironing shirts at the

sewing machine store, helping his dad stay on the sales floor by doing laundry in the back.

To this day, on the rare nights when I stay over at my parents' place, my dad insists on ironing my clothes. Stumbling to the bathroom at six in the morning, I'll see the faint silhouette of my dad pressing my dress shirt in the upstairs hallway before I leave for work.

It always makes me smile.

I've seen only one picture of my dad as a child, and it's a blurry black-and-white shot of him standing beside a bicycle with one of his older brothers.

Tall socks, flat faces, and neatly combed hair give a quick glimpse into a simple childhood full of big dreams. My dad loved math and eventually abandoned Charles Dickens to scrape together his savings, tutor in the evenings, and ride his bike to the University of Delhi for five years until he got his master's in nuclear physics in 1966. After university my dad applied for Canadian immigration and was accepted.

When I asked him why he applied to Canada, he said, "I looked up a ranking of the best places to live. Scandinavian countries were first but didn't accept immigrants. Canada and the US were next. So I applied to both. And I got the letter of acceptance from Canada first."

Just like a kid applying to colleges.

The reason his entire life and my entire life exist in Canada is just because he got the letter from Canada first.

How many big decisions have you made just because you got that letter first?

Are you checking your phone right now? I'm guessing there are three social media apps with notification flags waiting to hook your attention away. These days, we're surrounded by endless distractions. Never mind the twenty-three kinds of toothpaste and fourteen kinds of toilet paper you have to choose from on your drugstore pit stop on the way home.

There is magic in doing things simply.

In doing things *easily*.

Without all the thinking, thinking, thinking we apply to every single decision today.

How about this one?

First country you get a letter from?

Move there for the rest of your life.

2

They're not wrong. You're not right.

'm not the only one advocating for keeping decisions simple.

Harvard professor Daniel Gilbert, who we discussed earlier, calls this "the unanticipated joy of being totally stuck." He shows that the decisions we come to regard as *better* decisions are the ones we believe we didn't have a choice in. And if we did have a choice? Then we're prone to second-guessing ourselves. Doubt, wonder, and what-ifs all start seeping in. Likewise, Barry Schwartz, the author of *The Paradox of Choice*, observes that "though modern Americans have more choice than any group of people ever has before, and thus, presumably, more freedom and autonomy, we don't seem to be benefiting from it psychologically."

What decisions in your life are you overthinking?

I get we all want to maximize. We need to maximize! We have to maximize. The best date! The best party! The best school! The best house!

But if you think you could like either option of what you're choosing between . . . well, just pick one.

Tell yourself you don't have a choice.

And never, never stop.

In my dad's case, he thought he would like Canada or the US and the Canada letter came first.

So he arrived in Toronto with eight dollars in his pocket, which he spent in the first couple days.

My dad got a job as the first high school physics teacher in the local school district. "Physics is the king of the sciences," he'd say with a smile. And he even looked like a physicist, too, with wavy black hair, thick, long sideburns, and big boxy glasses. I sometimes thought of him as a bit of an Indian Einstein.

Sideburns have never gone out of style with my dad. He is more ruthlessly indifferent to fashion than anyone I know. Even when Jason Priestley and Luke Perry repopularized long side-burns on *Beverly Hills 90210* and suddenly every high school kid who could grow them was sporting big burns, did my dad chop his off? No, he just spent a random year *on trend*.

My dad lives by the book. He's the guy driving the speed limit on the highway in the right lane with everybody passing him the entire time. Nobody else is going the speed limit.

When we were kids, we used to make fun of him and tell him to drive faster and he'd say, "What happens if we get there five minutes earlier?" His plan was always to leave five minutes earlier and drive the speed limit.

My dad's the guy who tells the cashier she gave him an extra quarter back by mistake.

And his honesty sure did make him terrible at board games.

My family loved playing board games together but my dad

never got the hang of them. He was worst at Monopoly. He could roll the dice, move the boot, but he never won. Why? Because if he landed on your property and you forgot to charge him rent, he'd tell you.

He'd have his $20 ready and hand it over proudly as if to say, "Thank you! Thank you for letting me stay at your fine green house on Baltic Avenue."

"Dad," we'd say, shaking our heads. "If we forget to charge you rent, don't tell us. That's how you get more money! That's how you win the game!"

But he didn't get that.

He'd say, "If I stay at a property you own, I should pay my rent. And then you would pay me if you landed on mine, and we'd all be a lot happier instead of trying to trick each other all the time like you guys do."

My dad was trying to teach us something.

He was always trying to teach us something.

Because, more than anything, that's what he was: a teacher.

When I'd bring home my math or physics textbook and have trouble figuring out my homework, my dad would pull up a chair beside me and try to show me how to do it. When I still didn't understand, he would try again, except this time he would try teaching me a different way. If I didn't get it, he'd change again, and then he'd change again, and again, and again, until I, like any of the thousands of students he taught, finally figured it out.

He never, never stopped.

He's like one of those toy cars where you pull the wheels back and when it hits a wall it just turns and goes a different way.

There is something about that.

We live in an age where if somebody doesn't understand us, we show impatience, frustration, or surprise. We say it again. We yell! We pound our fists! We say it slower. So when somebody doesn't just repeat things, *but changes what they say*, you know they have a different view. It's not that *you're* not getting it. It's that *it's* hard to get. And the responsibility shifts to the person who's trying to explain.

I know I need to get better at remembering that *it's not on them* if somebody doesn't get what I'm saying. It's on me.

That's the root of real empathy.

My dad never raised his voice or got impatient. He never made you feel slow because you weren't catching on. He just kept changing how he taught you until his message got through.

In a way, all we're ever doing is seeing things, learning things, trying things in new ways.

And beyond never never stopping, my dad believed that *no type of learning was off limits*. He explained mortgage rates to me when I was three. He explained life insurance to me when I was four. And I can clearly remember asking him about the stock market when I was five or six years old. I was mesmerized by all the pages in the newspaper with the tiny little writing in columns. As always, he saw a learning opportunity and made a game of it with me.

"What's something you like?" he asked me.

"Um, Coke!" I answered.

"Okay," he said. "Look here. See this KO in the newspaper. That's Coca-Cola. It's $50. For $50, you can buy a share of

Coca-Cola. That means you can own some of the company. Do you want to buy some?"

Of course I did! I had some money saved up, so I gave it to my dad, and he bought me a couple shares of Coca-Cola.

My dad and I bought a big piece of poster board and we made a line graph of the Coca-Cola share price on the left side with the dates at the bottom. He taught me how to check the stock price every day and then I'd keep track of how much my stock was worth. I couldn't believe when the stock went up and up and up. He got me hooked on the idea that money can actually grow if you put it in the right business.

Also: never underestimate demand for sugar water.

3

Every connection is an opportunity

My dad also had the belief that every situation was an oppor-tunity for connection, and he mastered the art of learning from strangers.

I remember standing with him in a lot of lines. We'd go to the bank or I'd go with him to get the oil changed. There were more lines back then, more waiting. And no matter where we were, my dad always struck up a conversation with anybody around him to sort of break them out of the monotony. He'd get the bank teller laughing or have a three-minute sidebar with the waitress about the local sports team. If you wanted to talk stocks, my dad would talk stocks. If you wanted to talk movies, my dad would talk movies. If you wanted to talk about Margaret Thatcher, car maintenance, or gold prices, my dad would talk about those, too.

He always found some quick connection between himself and a stranger. Usually he made a little guess. "Saving for col-lege?" he'd ask. Or "Watching your kids?" or whatever it was. If they were game to play, then one nod led to two and I watched him time after time, year after year, turn those connections into little moments of beauty that brought out the best in people.

One of my most passionate projects today is my podcast *3 Books*. I get to chat with my heroes about books! I've sat down with Judy Blume and talked about why books need more sex scenes, with Mitch Albom about what matters in life after you've found meaning and purpose, and with David Sedaris about what drives the deep-seeded desire many of us have to always want more. I should be nervous having these chats. And I am! But I also know that every time I sit down, I am less nervous because I had a few decades of experience watching my dad.

I also watched his relentlessly curious mind share information that wasn't well known and ask for information back. It was a game he always played. It was like Trust Tradesies. He saw the machinations of industry and the economy all around him and always wondered why, how much, and could we?

So he'd say to the lady running the diner, "Rent at a restaurant like this is what, $8 a square foot? My niece pays $10 down the street, but she's on a corner." And then when she'd tell him what she paid, he'd do the math with me. "Look at the ceiling tiles. They're two feet by four feet. Count them across and down. What did you get? Right, so it's 1,600 square feet total, and at around $8 a square foot, that means they pay $13,000 a year for rent, right?"

He'd keep going, playing with the numbers, always simple

math, always in service of a larger point. "They probably have to serve fifty lunches a day to make money," he'd say. "That's a lot of meatloaf! That's hard work. I don't think we could do it."

Always, always ask.

Never, never stop.

4

You can only go forward

My dad knew only one direction. Forward.

When I was growing up, I'd ask him if we would ever go back to India and visit whatever distant second cousins or great aunts and uncles he had there.

"You go ahead," he'd say. "I'll fly to Miami and go on a cruise."

His idea of pleasure was baked Alaska served with a twinkling sea out the little porthole window. His memories of India were congestion, pollution, and poverty. He wasn't interested in going back physically—and he wasn't interested in going back mentally, either.

So we never visited.

Forward.

He knew what was worth worrying about and what wasn't.

He knew what was important and what wasn't.

He knew what was essential and that was to just keep moving forward.

When I struggle, when I hit a wall, when I get fired, when I miss a chance, when I feel like I wake up in the morning and am starting from scratch again . . . I think of my dad and his one-direction-only motto.

It's the final step to remember on the path to awesome.

The fact is we can only ever really go forward.

So the point is to just start going that way.

And never, never stop.

ADD A DOT-DOT-DOT

SHIFT THE SPOTLIGHT

SEE IT AS A STEP

TELL YOURSELF A DIFFERENT STORY

LOSE MORE TO WIN MORE

REVEAL TO HEAL

FIND SMALL PONDS

GO UNTOUCHABLE

NEVER, NEVER STOP

ACKNOWLEDGMENTS

aardvarks, Shawn Achor, Vishwas Aggrawal, Ajay Agrawal, Airplane Mode, Mitch Albom, Roberto Alomar, Chris Anderson, Deepak Angl, anyone who doesn't put ads on their stuff, Roger Ashby, Astro Boy, Bar Raval, Cameron Barr, Dave Barry, Aussie Bear, Beck, Pat Belmonte, Plezzie Benitez, Jen Bergstrom, birds, Ariel Bissett, Matt Blair, Gale Blank, Tracey Bloom, Judy Blume, Alan Blundell, Michal Bobinski, Sam Bradley, Darren Brehm, Scott Broad, Brené Brown, Ivana Budin, Ryan Buell, George Burford, bus drivers who drop you off right at your house, Keith Bussey, David Cain, Susan Cain, sugar cane, Jeremy Cammy, Joseph Campbell, Jenny Canzoneri, Holli Catchpole, Francesco Cefalu, the Center for Humane Technology, Clare Cheesewright, David Cheesewright, David Cheung, David Chilton, the Cooperstown Rejects, Wayne Coyne, Alec Crawford, Creeds, Crystal Pepsi, Roger Cude, Jim Davis, Rob Deeming, Tony D'Emidio, Marilyn Denis, Melvil Dewey, Guilherme Dias, Jeff Dinski, Siobhan Doody, Stella Dorsman, Mike Dover, Drew Dudley, Shera Eales, Kaye Egan, Amy Einhorn, the ellipsis . . . , Epictetus, Christine Farrell, Jonathan Fields, Tom Fitzsimmons, James Frey, Rich Gibbons, Malcolm Gladwell, Cassie Glasgow, Seth Godin, *Golden Words*, Robin Goodfellow, Kevin Groh, Chris Guillebeau, Bob Hakeem, Mohsin Hamid, Kevin Hanson, Kevin Hanson, Ryan Harper, *Harper's*, Michael Harris, Ivan Held, Ms. Hill, Ryan Holiday, Pete Holmes, Jerry Howarth, Kait Howell, Mr. Howes, Andrew Hughson, Hula, Humble The Poet, Mike Huntington, Paul Hunyor, Jason James, Mitch Joel, Stephen Johnson, Gary Johnston, Mike Jones, Satish Kanwar, Mitchell Kaplan, Chris Kim, Ms. King, Austin Kleon,

Kerri Kolen, Jon Krashinsky, Shivani Lakhanpal, Gary Larson, David Lavin, Joey Lee, Manny Lee, Eleanor LeFave, Jim Levine, Jim Levine, The Lexster, Andrew Limmert, Amanda Lindhout, Garry Liu, Beth Lockley, Kurt Luchs, Erik Lundgren, M83, Shelley Macbeth, Mr. Macdonald, Stephen Malkmus, Erin Malone, Mark Manson, Karyn Marcus, Drew Marshall, Elan Mastai, Agostino Mazzarelli, Gillian McClare, McDonald's, Emily McDowell, Janice McIntyre, Doug McMillon, Baxter Merry, Neil Meyers, Mike from BMV, David Mitchell, Brad Montague, Tracy Moore, Sophia Muthuraj, Krishna Nikhil, Danielle Nowakowski, Conan O'Brien, Mr. Olson, Brian Palmer, Sofi Papamarko, The Papercutters, Park & Province, Matt Parker, Shane Parrish, Adrian Pasricha, Akash Pasricha, Ken Pasricha, Nina Pasricha, Sunita Pasricha, Tamin Pechet, Cam Penman, Jen Penman, Farah Perelmuter, Martin Perelmuter, André Perold, Jay Pinkerton, Microsoft PowerPoint, Nita Pronovost, Nita Pronovost, Queen Street West, Felicia Quon, Sarah Ramsey, Heather Ranson, Blaise Ratcliffe, really fresh and chunky and salty and cold guacamole, Heather Reisman, An Richardson, Donna Richardson, Karen Richardson, Leslie Richardson, Leslie Richardson, Leslie Richardson, Mara Richardson, Mark Richardson, Rippy, Mel Robbins, Mike Robertson, Rich Roll, Michele Romanow, Gretchen Rubin, Ian Sabbag, Navraj Sagoo, Holly Santandreas, Conrad Schickedanz, Schuster, Jessica Scott, Section A, David Sedaris, *Seekers*, Ms. Selby, Seneca, Mariette Sequeira, Brian Shaw, Rita Silva, Simon, Simon & Schuster, Derek Sivers, Justin Skinner, Lesley Smith, Lauren Spiegel, Michael Bungay Stanier, Trey Stone, strangers who make funny faces at babies, Rita Stuart, Amit Taneja, Sumeer Taneja, Nassim Taleb, Kate Taylor, Ryan Taylor, the 2019 NBA Champion Toronto Raptors, all those teachers who work so hard just because they love their students and want to make a difference in their lives even though they get basically nothing for it, Freddo Thate, Ron Tite, Adrian Tomine, Toshi Auntie, trees, Brent Underwood, Chad Upton, Tim Urban, Gary Urda, David Foster Wallace, Michele Wallace, Sydne Waller, Frank Warren, water, Bill Watterson, Westy, Tom Wolfe, Bob Wright, Joan Wright, and zebras.

SOURCES

Introduction

Denizet-Lewis, Benoit. "Why Are More American Teenagers than Ever Suffering from Severe Anxiety?" *New York Times*, October 11, 2017.

Secret 1

Brannigan, Tania. "China's Great Gender Crisis." *Guardian*, November 2, 2011. https://www.theguardian.com/world/2011/nov/02/chinas-great-gender-crisis.

Brink, Susan. "Goats and Soda: Selecting Boys over Girls Is a Trend in More and More Countries." NPR, August 26, 2015. http://www.npr.org/sections/goatsandsoda/2015/08/26/434616512/selecting-boys-over-girls-is-a-trend-in-more-and-more-countries.

"Dowry." Wikipedia. Last modified April 23, 2019. https://en.wikipedia.org/wiki/Dowry.

"Code of Hammurabi." Wikipedia. Last modified April 30, 2019. https://en.wikipedia.org/wiki/Code_of_Hammurabi

Mahalik, James R., Elisabeth B. Morray, Aimée Coonerty-Femiano, Larry H. Ludlow, Suzanne M. Slattery, and Andrew

Smiler. "Development of the Conformity to Feminine Norms Inventory." *Sex Roles* 58, nos. 7/8 (April 2005). https://pdfs .semanticscholar.org/b10e/2703efb7fd9558e81866d14606b 0f2abeb30.pdf.

Shin, Jiwoong, and Dan Ariely. "Keeping Doors Open: The Effect of Unavailability on Incentives to Keep Options Viable." *Management Science* (May 2004). http://citeseerx.ist.psu.edu /viewdoc/download?doi=10.1.1.580.954&rep=rep1&type =pdf.

Secret 2

Huang, Karen, Alison Wood Brooks, Ryan W. Buell, Brian Hall, and Laura Huang. 2018. "Mitigating Malicious Envy: Why Successful Individuals Should Reveal Their Failures." Harvard Business School Working Paper, No. 18-080, February 2018. https://www.hbs.edu/faculty/Publication%20Files/18 –080_56688b05–34cd–47ef-adeb-aa7050b93452.pdf.

Keizer, Anouk, Monique A. M. Smeets, H. Chris Dijkerman, Siarhei A. Uzunbajakau, Annemarie van Elburg, Albert Postma, and Manos Tsakiris, eds. "Too Fat to Fit through the Door: First Evidence for Disturbed Body-Scaled Action in Anorexia Nervosa during Locomotion." *PLoS One* 8, no. 5 (May 2013). https://www.ncbi.nlm.nih.gov/pmc/articles /PMC3667140/.

"Scouts Seek Models at Swedish Anorexia Clinic." *The Local*, April 18, 2013. https://www.thelocal.se/20130418/47404# .UXABgitg8yE.

Breslaw, Anna. "Sad: Anorexics Try To 'Squeeze' Through Doorways They Could Easily Walk Through." *Cosmopolitan*, June

12, 2013. https://www.cosmopolitan.com/health-fitness /news/a13221/anorexia-squeeze-doorways-study/.

Gilovich, Thomas and Kenneth Savitsky. "The Spotlight Effect and the Illusion of Transparency: Egocentric Assessments of How We Are Seen by Others." *Current Directions in Psychological Science* 8 (6) (December 1, 1999): 165–168. https:// journals.sagepub.com/doi/10.1111/1467–8721.00039.

Starecheski, Laura. "Why Saying Is Believing—The Science of Self-Talk." *Morning Edition*, NPR, October 7, 2014. https:// www.npr.org/sections/health-shots/2014/10/07/353 292408/why-saying-is-believing-the-science-of-self-talk.

Secret 3

Quoidbach, Jordi, Daniel T. Gilbert, and Timothy D. Wilson. "The End of History Illusion." *Science* 339, no. 6115 (2013): 96–98. http://science.sciencemag.org/content/339/6115/96.

Tierney, John. "Why You Won't Be the Person You Expect to Be." *New York Times,* January 3, 2013. https://www.nytimes .com/2013/01/04/science/study-in-science-shows-end-of -history-illusion.html.

Miller, Greg. "Your Elusive Future Self." *Science,* January 3, 2013. https://www.sciencemag.org/news/2013/01/your-elusive -future-self.

Vedantam, Shankar. "You vs. Future You; Or Why We're Bad at Predicting Our Own Happiness." *Hidden Brain*, NPR, August 23, 2016. Audio, 24:1. https://www.npr.org/templates/tran script/transcript.php?storyId=490972873.

"Average woman will kiss 15 men and be heartbroken twice before meeting 'The One,' study reveals." *Telegraph*, January 1, 2014.

https://www.telegraph.co.uk/news/picturegalleries/how
aboutthat/10545810/Average-woman-will-kiss-15-men
-and-be-heartbroken-twice-before-meeting-The-One
-study-reveals.html

Secret 4

"Shame." *Lexico Online, powered by Oxford.* https://www.lexico
.com/en/definition/shame. Accessed June 21, 2019.

Mahalik, James R., Benjamin D. Locke, Larry H. Ludlow, Matthew
A. Dieme, Ryan P. J. Scott, Michael Gottfried, Gary Freitas.
"Development of the Conformity to Masculine Norms Inventory." *Psychology of Men & Masculinity* 4, no. 1 (2003): 3–25.
http://www.psychwiki.com/dms/other/labgroup/Measu
235sdgse5234234resWeek2/Krisztina2/Mahalik2003.pdf.

Brown, Brené. "Shame v. Guilt." Brené Brown, LLC. January 14,
2013. https://brenebrown.com/blog/2013/01/14/shame-v
-guilt/.

Brown, Brené. "Listening to Shame." Filmed March 2, 2012, in
Long Beach California. TED video, 20:32. https://www
.ted.com/talks/brene_brown_listening_to_shame/tran
script#t-1219024.

Golden, Bernard. *Overcoming Destructive Anger.* Baltimore: Johns
Hopkins University Press, 2016.

Heshmat, Shahram. "5 Factors That Make You Feel Shame." *Psychology Today,* October 4, 2015. https://www.psychologyto
day.com/us/blog/science-choice/201510/5-factors-make
-you-feel-shame.

Sznycer, Daniel, John Tooby, Leda Cosmides, Roni Porat, Shaul
Shalvi, and Eran Halperin. "Shame Closely Tracks the Threat

of Devaluation by Others, Even across Cultures." *Proceedings of the National Academy of Sciences* 113, no. 10 (March 2016): 2625–2630. http://www.pnas.org/content/113/10/2625.

Rhinehart, Luke. *The Book of est.* New York: Holt, Rinehart and Winston, 1976.

Dweck, Carol S. *Mindset: The New Psychology of Success.* New York: Penguin Random House LLC, 2006.

Steiner, Susie. "Top Five Regrets of the Dying." *Guardian*, February 1, 2012. https://www.theguardian.com/lifeandstyle/2012/feb/01/top-five-regrets-of-the-dying.

Secret 5

Sacks, Mike. *And Here's the Kicker: Conversations with 21 Top Humor Writers on Their Craft.* Cincinnati: Writer's Digest Books, 2009.

Godin, Seth. Interviewed by Tim Ferris. "Seth Godin on How to Say 'No,' Market Like a Professional, and Win at Life." *The Tim Ferris Show.* November 1, 2018.

Godin, Seth. Interviewed by Jonathan Fields. "Seth Godin: Learn to See, Leave Them Changed." *Good Life Project.* November 13, 2018.

Manson, Mark. *The Subtle Art of Not Giving a F*ck.* New York: HarperCollins, 2016.

Forleo, Marie. How to Stop Caring About Things that Don't Matter [Episode 41]. *The Marie Forleo Podcast.* https://podcasts.apple.com/ca/podcast/the-marie-forleo-podcast/id1199977889.

Secret 6

Bullard, Gabe. "The World's Newest Major Religion: No Religion." *National Geographic*, April 22, 2016. http://news.na tionalgeographic.com/2016/04/160422-atheism-agnostic -secular-nones-rising-religion/.

Twenge, Jean M., Julie J. Exline, Joshua B. Grubbs, Ramya Sastry and W. Keith Campbell. "Generational and Time Period Differences in American Adolescents' Religious Orientation, 1966–2014" *PLoS One* 10, no 5 (2015). https://journals.plos .org/plosone/article?id=10.1371/journal.pone.0121454.

Murthy, Vivek. "Work and the Loneliness." *Harvard Business Review*, September 17, 2018.

Brassen, Stefanie, Matthias Gamer, Jan Peters, Sebastian Gluth, and Christian Büchel. "Don't Look Back in Anger! Responsiveness to Missed Chances in Successful and Nonsuccessful Aging." *Science* 336, no. 6081 (May 4, 2012): 612–614. http:// science.sciencemag.org/content/336/6081/612.

Baumeister, Roy and John Tierney. *Willpower: Rediscovering The Greatest Human Strength*. New York: Penguin Group, 2011.

Schulte, Brigid. "Do These Exercises for Two Minutes a Day and You'll Immediately Feel Happier, Researchers say." *Washington Post*, June 29, 2015. https://www.washingtonpost.com /news/inspired-life/wp/2015/06/29/do-these-exercises-for -two-minutes-a-day-and-youll-immediately-feel-happier -researchers-say/?utm_term=.fbc3f4b364b2.

Secret 7

Marsh, H. W., and J. W. Parker. (1984) "Determinants of student self-concept: Is it better to be a relatively large fish in a small pond even if you don't learn to swim as well? *Journal of Personality and Social Psychology* 47, no. 1 (1984): 213–231. http://dx.doi.org/10.1037/0022–3514.47.1.213.

"Big-fish-little-pond effect." Wikipedia. Last modified May 6, 2018. https://en.wikipedia.org/wiki/Big-fish%E2%80%93little-pond_effect.

Secret 8

Schwartz, Alexandra. "Improving Ourselves to Death." *New Yorker*, January 8, 2018. https://www.newyorker.com/magazine/2018/01/15/improving-ourselves-to-death.

Wu, Tim. "In Praise of Mediocrity." *New York Times*, September 29, 2018. https://www.nytimes.com/2018/09/29/opinion/sunday/in-praise-of-mediocrity.html.

Leroy, Sophie. "Why Is It So Hard to Do My Work? The Challenge of Attention Residue When Switching between Work Tasks." *Organizational Behavior and Human Decision Processes* 109, no. 2 (July 2009): 168–181. https://www.sciencedirect.com/science/article/pii/S0749597809000399.

Secret 9

Gilbert, Daniel. *Stumbling on Happiness.* New York: Random House, 2006.

Schwartz, Barry. "The Paradox of Choice." Filmed July 2005 in Oxford, UK. TED video, 19:37. https://www.ted.com/talks/barry_schwartz_on_the_paradox_of_choice.

ABOUT THE AUTHOR

LEIA VITA

NEIL PASRICHA thinks, writes, and speaks about intentional living. He is the *New York Times* bestselling author of six books, including *The Book of Awesome* and *The Happiness Equation*, which have spent over 200 weeks on bestseller lists and have sold over a million copies. He hosts the award-winning podcast *3 Books*, where he's on a fifteen-year quest to uncover the thousand most formative books in the world by interviewing people such as Malcolm Gladwell, Angie Thomas, and the world's greatest Uber driver. He gives more than fifty speeches a year, appearing for audiences at places such as TED, SXSW, and Google. He has degrees from Queen's University and Harvard Business School and lives in Toronto with his wife Leslie and their three sons. Connect with him on social media **@neilpasricha**, visit him at **Neil.blog**, or drop him a line at **neil@globalhappiness.org**.